AN INTRODUCTION TO PRIMARY EDUCATION

FOR PARENTS, GOVERNORS AND STUDENT TEACHERS

Andrew Pollard

CASSELL

Cassell
Wellington House, 125 Strand, London WC2R 0BB
215 Park Avenue South, New York, NY 10003

First published 1996

British Library Cataloguing-in-Publication Data
A catalogue record for this book is available from the British Library

ISBN 0–304–32710–7 (hardback)
ISBN 0–304–32708–5 (paperback)

Typeset by Chapter One (London)
Printed and bound in Great Britain by
Redwood Books, Trowbridge, Wiltshire

EDUCATION MATTERS

General Editor: Ted Wragg

AN INTRODUCTION TO PRIMARY EDUCATION

CONTENTS

FOREWORD

Professor E. C. Wragg, Exeter University

During the 1980s a succession of Education Acts changed considerably the nature of schools and their relationships with the outside world. Parents in particular were given more rights and responsibilities, including the opportunity to serve on the governing body of their child's school. The 1988 Education Reform Act, by introducing for the first time a National Curriculum, the testing of children at 7, 11, 14 and 16, local management including financial responsibility, and the creation of new types of school, was a radical break with the past.

In the wake of such rapid and substantial changes it was not just parents and lay people, but also teachers and other professionals who found themselves struggling to keep up with what these changes meant and how to get the best out of them. The *Education Matters* series addresses directly the major topics of reform – the new curriculum, testing and assessment, the role of parents and the handling of school finances – considering their effects on both primary and secondary education.

The aim of the series is to present information about the challenges facing education in the remainder of the twentieth century in an authoritative but readable form. The books in the series, therefore, are of particular interest to parents, governors and all those interested in education, but are written in such a way as to give an overview of student and experienced teachers or other professionals in the field.

Each book gives an account of the relevant legislation and background, but, more importantly, stresses the practical implications of change with specific examples of what is being or can be done to make reforms work effectively. The authors of each book are not only authorities in their field, but also have direct experience of the matters they write about, and that is why the *Education Matters* series makes an important contribution to both debate and practice.

ACKNOWLEDGEMENTS

I would like to thank the children, teachers and parents who contributed to the contents of this book and to Dorothy Abbott, Ian Menter and Will Pollard who kindly read the manuscript in draft and offered constructive criticisms.

Sarah Butler, with her immense efficiency, was responsible for the production of this text and I am grateful to her.

I am also grateful to Neville Bennett and Falmer Press for permission to reproduce Figure 4.1, and to officials of SCAA and ACAC for advice on the synopsis of the National Curriculum.

Andrew Pollard,
University of Bristol

PREFACE

This book has been written for parents, governors and student teachers.

Building on my previous book, *Learning in Primary Schools*, my intention was to provide a straightforward, but principled and informed guide to primary education as we move towards the millennium. Thus, all the most important issues are covered: teaching and learning, pupils, parents, teachers and governors, curriculum, pedagogy, assessment, resources, school management and inspection.

However, woven among this comprehensive coverage is a main theme. This is a simple commitment to try to look at each issue from the point of view of children as learners. Thus, as we deal with each topic, the question will be posed, 'How does this affect pupils and their learning?'.

Additionally, the new book offers resources to provide information about the content of the National Curriculum and to assist in understanding the numerous influences, issues and concepts which affect primary education. You should therefore try 'putting the book to work', and use the compendium, cross-referencing, indexing, suggestions for further reading and explanations in the main text to explore the issues with which you are concerned.

The book is structured in two parts: 'Learning in primary schools' and 'Resources for understanding primary edcation'.

'Part One: Learning in primary schools', begins with a chapter in which three common ways of thinking about children's learning are introduced. Since learning is the main theme of the book as a whole, this is an important chapter. Chapter 2 is focused on schools as children and parents experience them, whilst Chapter 3 provides a concise introduction to the background, structure and content of the National Curriculum and associated assessment procedures.

Chapters 4, 5 and 6 form a group in that they deal with the main adult groups who structure children's lives – teachers, parents, governors and headteachers. In each case the chapters focus on the question of how these people can contribute most beneficially to the learning process. Chapter 6 also focuses on other, more general, issues in school management and considers school accountability and school inspection.

In the final chapter of this part, Chapter 7, I address some wider issues and review the challenges which face primary education as we begin to move into the twenty-first century. Indeed, the full consequences of new systems of management, accountability, curriculum and assessment, introduced in the late 1980s and early 1990s, are still emerging. I conclude that parents, governors and teachers share a common commitment to the quality of learning and experience of young children and that, potentially, they constitute a powerful alliance which can promote and enhance children's interests.

'Part Two: Resources for understanding primary education', offers two chapters of useful information.

Chapter 8 is a simple compendium of influences, issues and concepts which are important in the thinking, language and practice of primary education. It is intended to be used for reference purposes and is fully cross-referenced to the main text.

Chapter 9 provides a synopsis of the National Curriculum for primary schools in England and Wales. The situation in Scotland, Northern Ireland and elsewhere is rather different, although interestingly there is evidence from across the world of considerable convergence of national curricula in the post-war years (Meyer *et al.*, 1992).

Every chapter in Part 1 ends with suggestions for further reading and the book concludes with an integrated bibliography and a full index.

If you wish to delve in greater detail, a more advanced book which can be used in a similar way to this one is:

Pollard, A. and Tann, S. (1993) *Reflective Teaching in the Primary School*. London: Cassell.

INTRODUCTION

From their first movements and cries on the day they are born each child begins to acquire skills, and knowledge which will equip them as an adult. Parents and the home are undoubtedly the most important influences. As parents, setting the hard work aside, we wonder at the speed of our childrens' physical development, delight in their struggles to understand and derive enormous pleasure from their achievements – from their sitting to walking and on, through the pivotal ability of talking, to such abilities as running, singing, or even eating with a bit less mess. Through all of these experiences, their uniqueness as people grows.

Young children also exhibit a full range of emotions and this is, itself, a source of considerable parental pleasure as well as occasional annoyance. Do you remember your child's first smile, their expressions of excitement, the sound of their laughter – and of their anger? Whatever form their emergent character might take, we must never forget that young children share and deserve the rights, dignity and respect which are due to each of us – an injunction which must be applied to schools as much as to any other influence on children's lives.

By the time children are 5 years old and thus reach what, in the UK, is school age, they have already developed, experienced and learned an enormous amount. Thus, each 5-year-old who enters school will present the emergent personality which develops further with them throughout their lives. As parents, we have to recognize and accept that such characteristics are likely to reflect much of ourselves. Just as we become the people we are through our lives, so it is for our children.

Children, of course, do not generally think in such terms. They tend to be bound up in the immediacy of the present. At the same time though they tell us a great deal about themselves and this is knowledge on which we may ground our optimism for the future. Consider the example of a child's writing in Figure I.1 It began life simply as a piece of scrap paper from a school classroom – and it then became a note from 'Naomi to Miss' conveying important news from a 5-year-old about her new shoes and how she felt about them. For those who are not too sure, the note says:

'I'm happy, I'm happy,
I know I am. I'm sure I am.
I'm happy because I got new shoes!'

So what does this illustrate? I would suggest the following:

- the intense, special and trusting relationship which often grows up between teacher and child (the excitement of the shoes which has to be shared);
- the delight of young children in their own development, (the smile, the meaning and almost poetic quality of the writing);
- the achievements of which even young children are capable, given confidence, skill and a little knowledge (consider the skill and knowledge about writing which is shown here following the instruction offered by Naomi's parents and teacher);
- the ingenuity of primary school teachers in bringing available resources into their classrooms to make up for the relatively low levels of funding for primary-aged pupils (it looks as if a job lot of old building society paper has been used here);
- the disarming freshness, openness and eager engagement of young children which can be a constant source of positive feedback and fulfilment for adults;
- the importance of trusting relationships and a caring environment to support children's learning. (Naomi *wants* to communicate with her teacher – and she doesn't expect her note to come back with the spelling, grammar and layout corrected in red pen, but with no comment on the message. She feels able to take the risks involved in trying things out, even through writing. She has opened herself to the process of learning.)

Figure I.1 Naomi's note to her teacher

All these ideas are part of themes which will be developed throughout the book. The focus is on children learning through their primary education and on the ways in which adults and schools can facilitate their efforts. We will not be able to forget, however, that the relationships, openness and risk-taking involved in learning often render the learner rather vulnerable. In a mass system of primary education, where classes normally contain between 25 and 30 children, this is an important issue. How can teachers facilitate and enable the learning of each child? How do the structures of the National Curriculum and the national requirements for assessment support children's learning? Do adults look beyond the concerns of their busy lives to fully recognize children's capabilities? Many of these issues apply to home life as much as to life in school.

The ways in which primary schools approach learning and the ways in which parents and governors can support them will be a constant theme throughout this book. After all, learning is the reason for schooling and must remain the central concern of us all. However, it is very easy to lose sight of this simple fact particularly when we, as adults, experience or have responsibility for only a part of the education which is provided for each child. A teacher will have a different perspective from a governor or parent, and of course, even within these groups of people, there will be wide variations in beliefs and practices in learning.

For thousands of years people have developed without the benefit of formal education. Indeed, it is only since the early part of the nineteenth century that anything like a mass system for education outside the home began to emerge in Europe. This innovation was a product, both of the development of industrialization and of a rethinking of how people could influence their circumstances. The movements that arose are still with us and, in their modern forms, are manifest in high technology, sophisticated communication systems, mass production and, increasingly, in an international culture. The opportunities that modern societies afford are great, they have their downsides too. There are considerable differences in wealth and opportunity and, for many families, poverty is still a reality. Feelings, emotions and the arts must compete with pressures for economic efficiency. Environmental time-bombs continue to tick away and could threaten even more than just the *quality* of life.

So while we may take pleasure from our children, it is also clear that we very much need them. They are our most precious resource. They represent our collective future. It is no wonder that the education of young children attracts so much public attention.

Suggestions for further reading

On a regular basis, the coverage in three magazines is the best way to keep in touch:

Junior Education (which has a particularly good newsline)
Child Education (which is good for early years work)
Times Educational Supplement (which is the basic, multi-purpose, cross-phase magazine for the teaching profession)
A user-friendly, but more academic, journal is:
Education 3–13

Part One
LEARNING IN PRIMARY SCHOOLS

Chapter 1
CHILDREN LEARNING

Some people have suggested that the psychology of learning is too complex a topic to introduce into a book of this sort – a view which seems a little odd to me. After all, we are all learners, we all reflect on our experiences, talk to our friends and develop our thinking over time. Such everyday processes should not be dismissed lightly. What we must do, however, is to think carefully about them and to identify more explicitly how learning takes place. We can then recognize how we may affect the learning of young children ourselves.

Three well-worn sayings encompass much of what it is important to understand about childrens' learning. They are: 'Listen, and you will learn', 'You learn best by doing' and 'Let's discuss it'. I will rehearse the ideas which are associated with them below. In so doing I will clearly be guilty of all sorts of misrepresentations of the complexity of psychological work. However, the positions which I have highlighted do, in my view, reflect the essence of three significant forms of psychology as they affect education.

'Listen, and you will learn'

Such a confident and authoritative statement may be associated with the traditional, 'chalk and talk' form of teaching. In this approach the learner is seen as a *tabula rasa*; a passive, blank space into which knowledge is to be passed by a suitably qualified adult. As I was told in my schooldays, it is sometimes useful to 'read, mark, learn and inwardly digest' the subject-matter – be it spelling, poetry, multiplication tables or historical dates. When facts are well learned, they may be instantly recalled, though doubts exist about how well they, or more complex issues, may be understood. Knowledge tends to be seen in absolute terms by those who adopt this approach and this can cause problems for children who find such learning difficult. There is no doubt that children can and do learn much from listening to adults. The important point though is that the adult's offerings must be appropriate for the learner. They must be meaningful and they must connect with the knowledge and understanding which the learner already possesses.

Nevertheless, this approach, which I have portrayed as having an emphasis on 'listening' – an external adult-controlled stimulus – is securely underpinned by 'behaviourist psychology' which goes back many years to Pavlov and Skinner. Thus children learn by listening carefully to get the correct stimulus and through the repeated reinforcement of correct responses.

'You learn best by doing'

This second statement is closely related to a saying by Confucius, the philosopher of Ancient China, 'I do and I understand'. This encapsulates the essence of the philosophy of much primary education of the late 1960s and 1970s. The emphasis is on direct experience and on interaction with media, artefacts, people and places. Learners are seen as active – as 'doing' – and thereby constructing their understanding as they interact with the environment and the people and materials within it. However, in this model, the emphasis is on each learner as an individual – it is 'I' who 'does' and 'understands'. Such an active, investigating child is thus seen as being rather like the lone scientist, working rationally and progressively to build successive layers of understanding, skill and knowledge.

In this approach all children are positively valued for their individual gifts and potential. The task of the teacher or adult is seen as being to provide stimulating activities and a secure environment within which the child can grow and develop. Children should be nurtured, as with delicate plants, as they develop naturally through successive stages of intellectual development.

This emphasis on doing, on activity, and experience, is associated with the 'constructivist psychology' of Piaget. Children learn through interaction with their environment and both accommodate to it and assimilate what is to be learned from it. Through this progressive process, new 'stages' of thinking are reached and these, it is thought, define much of a child's needs and thinking capacities.

Both of the approaches considered above attribute importance to talk and language. However, it is the psychological approach known as 'social constructivism' which really gives priority to discussion as the major vehicle of learning.

'Let's discuss it'

Statements such as this imply learning through interaction between people. Once again the learner is active and knowledge has to be constructed rather than handed down. It is not absolute. However, in this model, learners are not alone and emphasis is placed on each child learning through engagement with other people – be they children or adults. Of course, the strong emphasis on discussion is underpinned by the experience of many people that talking with others is a very effective way of clarifying one's thinking.

This 'social constructivist' approach can be traced back to a Russian psychologist, Vygotsky, and has, in recent years, been particularly promoted by an American, Jerome Bruner. In particular, it has been shown that adult support for children in their thinking is vital. With an appropriate question, intervention or suggestion, the child's understanding can be extended far beyond the point which they could have reached alone. Thus, to use the exceptionally impressive jargon, the 'zone of proximal development' (ZPD) in the child's understanding can be crossed and the next intellectual step taken. Figure 1.1 may help to clarify this important process.

In this figure, the learning attainments which people achieve through life are represented as rising from a base to an infinite extent. Now imagine, say, a 5-year-old girl at the beginning of her time in school. At any point as she develops, there will be some things which she really does feel confident about, things she knows, can do and understands. I have labelled this level of confident attainment the 'zone of *existing* development', Zone A. At the other extreme, in Zone C, there are many areas

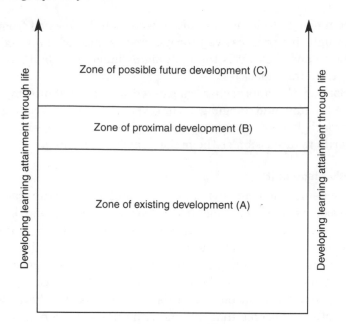

Figure 1.1 A representation of zones of learning development and attainment

of knowledge, capability and understanding which are likely to be too difficult for our imagined little girl. Were she to be presented with such challenges now, she might well become anxious and feel a sense of bewilderment or failure. However, they await her in the future and, one day, she may well reach such levels of attainment. What lies ahead of her is the 'zone of possible *future* development'.

The key area for making learning progress lies in Zone B, in what Vygotsky called the 'zone of *proximal* development'. This is the area which encompasses levels of learning attainment which the child could reach now, *if* she was given appropriate support and instruction.

A main challenge here lies in the adult sensitivity and skill which this implies. Providing 'appropriate help' is not at all easy, for not only must one be able to recognize what a child understands already and is motivated to learn, but one must also have the knowledge to help them, the skill to explain or provide instruction in appropriate ways, and the patience, tact and awareness to carry it off.

Such adult support is often referred to as providing 'scaffolding' for children's learning. It offers a temporary structure within which children construct their own understanding. To extend the analogy, we should note that no building can stand with scaffolding alone but each must have its own foundations, its own intrinsic stability and coherence. So it is with secure forms of understanding which, despite the initial role of external support, the learner must construct for themselves.

Of course, as successive learning attainments are reached, the range of each zone changes. Zone A of existing development grows and Zone C of future development continues to beckon. The crucial area for growth, always moving slightly ahead of the learner, remains the 'zone of proximal development'.

Having made these general points about levels of learning attainment, we must not forget that children can learn about a very wide range of topics *if* they are introduced to them in appropriate ways. Research shows that even young children search to understand issues such as poverty, conflict, pollution or violence, but they often do this without the support of those adults who regard childhood strictly as an age of innocence. The reality though is that children's innocence cannot be entirely protected any more than we can be confident about placing all knowledge, skill or understanding in some rank order or hierachy of difficulty. Adults need to support children's learning as their interests and motivations develop, and these may well be in unpredictable ways. Whatever the focus though, there will always be zones of confidence, zones of what is possible and zones of what is best left for the future. The adult role is to help the child to realize the possibilities and thus fulfil their potential.

Such adult interventions are, of course, enacted through social processes and, for this reason, awareness of the social factors which affect each child is particularly prominent in social constructivist thinking about learning. This draws attention to the family, friends and culture which influence each pupil beyond the school. He or she is not simply seen as an individual pupil but as a person in society. Thus it is assumed that the social context will have an effect on how children learn and, in due course, to affect how they think about themselves and how others treat them. In other words, it begins to affect their sense of identity. The next section offers an illustration of how such social and cultural processes work.

Learning and developing an identity

This illustration focuses on the educational experiences of two children who each attended a primary school in a suburb of a large city in England. They began their school careers together, along with 24 others, in the same 'reception' class.

Our first child, a girl called Sally, was the youngest of the two children of the school caretaker. Her mother also worked in the school as a school meals supervisory assistant and as a cleaner. Her parents had always taken enormous pleasure and pride in Sally's achievements. They celebrated each step as it came but did not seem to overtly press her in any way. Life, for them, seemed very much in perspective. Sally was physically agile and had a good deal of self-confidence. She had known the school and the teaching staff for most of her life. She felt at home. She was very sensitive to 'school rules' and adult concerns and she engaged in each new challenge with zest. Over the years, with her parents' encouragement, she had developed a considerable talent for dancing and had won several competitions. In school she had also taken a leading role in several class assemblies and had made good progress with her reading and other work. The teachers felt she was a delightful and rewarding child to teach – convivial and able, but compliant too. Her friends were mainly girls though she mixed easily. She was at the centre of a group which was particularly popular in the class and who, over the years since playgroup, had developed strong internal links and friendships through shared interests and visiting each other's homes.

The second child, Daniel, was the fifth and youngest in his family. His father was an extremely busy business executive and his mother had devoted the previous 16 years to caring for their children – a worthwhile but all-absorbing commitment.

She was concerned for Daniel who had had some difficulties in establishing his identity in the bustle of the family with four older children. She also felt that he had 'always tended to worry about things' and was not very confident in himself. For many years he had tended to play on being the youngest, the baby of the family, a role which seemed naturally available. At playgroup he was particularly friendly with a girl, Harriet, who was later to be in his class at school. However, over their first year at school, distinct friendships of boys and girls began to form. It became 'sissy' to play with girls. Daniel, who had found the transition from the security of home hard to take and who had to begin to develop a greater self-sufficiency, thus found the ground rules of appropriate friendships changing, as the power of child culture asserted itself. He could not play with Harriet because she was a girl, but nor was he fully accepted by the dominant groups of boys.

This insecurity was increased when he moved from the structured and motherly atmosphere of his reception class into the more volatile environment of his 'middle infant' class. There were now 31 children in his class, most of whom were from a parallel reception class – within which a group of boys had developed a reputation for being 'difficult'. The new teacher thus judged that the class 'needed a firm hand to settle them down after last year' and, as a caring but experienced infant teacher, decided to stand no nonsense. It also so happened that this teacher was somewhat stressed, as a lot of teachers were at the time. She thus sometimes acted in ways which were against her own better judgement.

The environment which Daniel experienced was thus one which which was sometimes a little unpredictable. Whilst he was never one of the ones who 'got into trouble', he was very worried by the possibility that he might 'upset Miss' and that she might 'get cross'. Daniel would thus be very careful. He would watch and listen to the teacher, attempting to 'be good' and do exactly what was required. He would check with other children and, on making a first attempt at a task, try to have his efforts approved before proceeding further. Occasionally, at work with a group and with other children also pressing, the teacher might wave Daniel away. He would then drift, unsure, watching to take another opportunity to obtain the reinforcement which he felt he needed. As the year progressed, Daniel became more unhappy and increasingly unwilling to go to school.

Daniel's mother was torn as this situation developed – was the 'problem' caused by Daniel's 'immaturity' or was it because he was frightened of the teacher? She felt it was probably a bit of both but school-gate advice suggested that discussion in school might not go easily. She delayed and the situation worsened, with Daniel making up excuses to avoid school, insisting on returning home for lunch and becoming unwilling to visit the homes of other children. Daniel's mother eventually and tentatively visited the school where the issues were aired.

Over the following weeks the teacher worked hard to support Daniel and to help him settle. Daniel's confidence improved a little, particularly when he found a new friend, a boy, from whom he then became inseparable. Even so, as his mother told me towards the end of the year, 'we are holding on and praying for the end of term'.

These two children attended the same school and were part of the same classes – yet as learners they had quite different characteristics. Whilst Sally was confident, keen to 'have a go' and would take risks, Daniel was insecure, fearful lest he 'got things wrong' in a world in which he felt evaluated and vulnerable. The accident of birth into a small or large family may have been an influence too, with Sally having had the psychological space to flourish and the day-to-day support of both her parents all around her, whilst Daniel had to establish his place in a large family in which both parents faced considerable pressure in their work – be it in an office or domestically. Perhaps too, Daniel's initial solutions to his position, which had carried him in good stead in his infancy, whilst at home, would simply not transfer into the less bounded environment of school.

Sally and Daniel certainly learned a lot from 'listening', 'doing' and 'discussing', with the support of many adults, but the story of these two children is not just about learning in a narrow academic sense. It is also about the ways in which Sally and Daniel began to develop their identities as people. Self-image and self-confidence develop alongside skills and knowledge and are particularly important in the primary school years. We must remember too that children have uneven patterns of development. Daniel may very well develop more poise and belief in himself as he gets older. He has already shown considerable ingenuity through his actions, albeit defensively deployed, and perhaps this will, in due course, be applied more directly to his learning.

The main points embedded in these two accounts are, I hope, clear:

- The way children approach learning tasks is influenced by home as well as school. Continuity is vital – but is not always easy to achieve.
- There are powerful social and emotional factors involved in learning. The learner must feel secure and able to take the risks which are involved in facing learning challenges within their zones of proximal development.
- The social context in which learning takes place is very important and will have an impact on children irrespective of their individual capabilities.
- There is no necessary connection between social class factors or income levels and the quality of the learning environment which parents can provide.

For learning to be effective in the long term, it is imperative that children develop a sense of perspective on what is involved. They need to be able to adopt a range of strategies – to make the most of their opportunities for listening, doing and discussing. Their capacity to do this is inextricably tied into their emerging sense of identity and will be manifested in the stance which they adopt to school life. Will they engage new challenges with relish? Will they guardedly play safe? Will they develop the capacities to judge what is appropriate when, with different people, at particular times and in specific situations?

Conclusion

In this chapter, I have introduced three commonplace sayings and indicated something of the psychological thinking to which they can be related. I have also discussed some of the reasons why each, though different, is thought to contain some elements of good sense about learning, and I summarize these in Table 1.1. The table also takes the analysis a little further by identifying the image of learners and the view of learning that are implied, and by suggesting some strengths and weaknesses of each approach.

Table 1.1   Some predominant features of listening, doing and discussing as a means of learning

	Listening	*Doing*	*Discussing*
Image of learner	• Passive • Individual	• Active • Individual	• Active • Social
Image of learning	• Passed down from adults	• Constructed gradually through stages of development	• Constructed gradually through children's interests and adult support
Some strengths	• Draws on existing knowledge	• Provides direct experience • Clarifies thinking	• Extends understanding • Clarifies thinking
Some weaknesses	• May not connect with existing understanding	• Has major resource and organizational implications	• Has major resource and organizational implications • A high level of adult skill and sensitivity is required

In the bustle of daily life it is clear that the analytical distinctions between, and the originators of, different sorts of psychology may not always be at the top of everyone's mind. However, being aware of some basic principles of learning becomes essential when we think about providing high-quality and internally consistent education for children. This is why I have raised the issues right at the start of this book.

In most primary schools, for instance, aspects of each of the three approaches to learning could be found. Sometimes this reflects history – for they are each associated with particular eras of precedence. Sometimes it simply reflects a poorly thought out form of provision, whilst in other cases it will reflect an accurate professional judgement and appropriate application of the strengths and weaknesses of the different approaches.

In case this sounds confusing, let me suggest that the basic test for every teacher, parent and governor should simply be in terms of children's experience. The children are at the centre of the whole schooling process. Adults structure their lives in so many ways and yet it is the children who must cope with the consequences of adult plans. Indeed, parents, teachers and governors bear very heavy responsibilities for children's learning because each child develops their perspectives and strategies in response to his or her need to cope with circumstances which we control. If we fail to co-operate, to liaise, to negotiate or to think our actions through, then it is the children who suffer. Their lives are, literally, an ongoing test of the continuity and support which we provide. Certainly such vulnerability deserves our attention and can, I would argue, best be addressed by focusing on the nature of the learning provision in different settings. That is why the theme of learning will recur throughout this book as we review the main elements which make up primary education.

Suggestions for further reading

There are two classic books on children's learning, the insights and accessibility of which have yet to be bettered:

Holt, J. (1965) *How Children Fail*. Harmondsworth: Penguin.

Holt, J. (1967) *How Children Learn*. Harmondsworth: Penguin.

For delightful insights into very young children's thinking see:

Paley, V. G. (1981) *Wally's Stories*. London: Harvard University Press.

Paley, V. G. (1990) *The Boy Who Would be a Helicopter*. London: Harvard University Press.

For more detailed treatment of the three psychological approaches to learning see Chapter 6 of:

Pollard, A. and Tann, S. (1993) *Reflective Teaching in the Primary School*. London: Cassell.

Two accessible but more academic texts are:

Wood, D. (1988) *How Children Think and Learn*. Oxford: Blackwell.

Bruner, J. S. (1990) *Acts of Meaning*. London: Harvard University Press.

Whilst Wood's book is an excellent review of the present state of knowledge, Bruner's volume offers the broad and cultured sweep of one of the most distinguished psychologists of the post-war years advocating a 'cultural psychology' – and all in an elegant prose. Highly recommended if you want to take the issues on at that level.

The full stories of Daniel and Sally are told and analysed, along with those of several other children, in:

Pollard, A. with Filer, A. (1995) *The Social World of Children's Learning*. London: Cassell.

Chapter 2
EXPERIENCING PRIMARY SCHOOLS

How does it feel if you happen to be a child going to primary school each day? Of course, at a detailed level there will be as many answers to such a question as there are people. There are many common factors however, and these provide the focus for this chapter. We start with a brief consideration of the impact of the physical environment of schools before addressing school ethos in a little more detail. Then we focus on children's experience of starting school and on their first year, before moving to discuss the ways in which schools structure children's lives more generally. We conclude with consideration of children's perspectives and friendships and of the 'child culture' they create.

'It's a big place, Mummy'

Primary schools have a particular significance for young children because they provide a main step towards the adult world and away from the security of home life. The familiarity of home is replaced by a far larger institution, new people to relate with, different rules and conventions and more specific goals to which each child must respond. The pride in 'starting school' thus tends to be counterbalanced by some anxiety about this strange new world, particularly for the large number of 4-year-old children who start in Reception classes each year. Then, of course, this new world constantly unfolds before each child as they 'move up' to successive teachers, year by year. 'Becoming a junior' is particularly significant, for official status in such terms seems, to children, to be almost as significant a sign of their growing independence as the loss of teeth. True, in the case of teeth, they will gratefully accept whatever may appear under their pillow, but the associated pleasure of such experiences is mainly to do with status – passage on the way to 'growing up'.

21

Children know that they must contend with the new physical environments which primary schools present. In this respect, the challenges may be very diverse, for there is enormous variety among primary schools in the UK. Some schools date from the last century – with high windows, imposing, vaulted halls and solid stone walls – many others are products of post-war building programmes with more glass, brick and flat roofs in evidence. Some are based on self-contained classrooms, others are open-plan. Many city schools are surrounded by tarmacked playgrounds and railings and have few grassed areas. Schools in the suburbs tend to have more grass and other sorts of play-space, whilst village schools vary again, depending on their history and endowment. The average primary school has just under 200 pupils and eight or nine teachers but, from rural village to inner-city community school the range of size and provision is breathtaking. And yet the particular size, architecture and environmental surroundings of each school are very significant to children's experience of school. A world of high windows, tiled corridors, concrete stairs and walled play-grounds is very different from one of light, space, courtyards, playing fields and trees. Of course, teachers in any situation will do their very best to make the school environment welcoming, interesting and secure but it is not always easy, particularly considering the inadequate sums which are often available for refurbishment or maintenance of buildings.

There are two questions which, I would suggest, might well be asked about a school environment. First, how is it likely to influence the children's feelings about school – their opportunities to play together, to experience a range of activities and to feel secure? Second, how is it likely to influence the teaching/learning process – the opportunities for listening, doing, talking and discussing in the school? Such questions are important, but, as we should all know, it is the people who really count.

The school ethos

At the heart of a good primary school, above and beyond its buildings, are its people and the sense of community which they try to engender. There are, undeniably, particular qualities in the impressions and feelings conveyed by each school – each has a climate or ethos which, hopefully, is one of welcome. However, each is unique to itself and, whatever form the ethos actually takes, it will have an enormous influence on how life in that school is experienced by the children.

A school ethos normally reflects an amalgam, negotiated over the years, of the values and beliefs of those who work in the school. In this, the influence of the headteacher is particularly important. Once it is established, the school ethos underpins and structures everything which is and is not acceptable to do. Both tacit and explicit rules and expectations flow from it and thus frame vital issues such as order and discipline, quality and standards of work, manners and behaviour.

Of course, a school ethos is at its most influential when people identify with it, when it reflects shared values and agreed commitments – particularly among teaching staff. However, a danger of complacency also exists in such circumstances and sometimes innovations such as the development of new ways of teaching and new curricula need to be introduced. Skilled headteachers will do their utmost to facilitate team-based development of the school with everyone constructively pulling together, but some tension is also possible. Indeed, research shows that schools tend to go through regular cycles of development, often with periods of rapid change on the appointment of a new head and a phase of maximum effectiveness when things have settled after a few years. Clearly, children's experience, in terms of the cohesion and consistency presented by the staff, is likely to be affected by the particular point which their school has reached in its cycle of development. Some schools have detailed, agreed and coherent approaches which have been soundly established. In some others there may be a degree of conflict and the children's experience, as they move from class to class, may reflect this.

There are many ways of finding out about a school ethos because it is at its most evident in public situations. You can thus see how the children go into and leave school, how they use the playground and, in particular, how they interact with teachers in school performances, assemblies and other events.

Such events usually rely for their smooth running on the existence of shared understandings among the school community
and reinforcement of these assumptions and ways of behaving
are often made overt. For instance, at one junior school which I
have often visited the headteacher has close relationships with
the children and loves to joke with them – as long as it doesn't
go too far! It has now almost become a tradition at each school
concert for him to introduce the massed choirs of children and
then retire behind the parents to the back of the hall. From
there he engenders row upon row of smiling, wholehearted
singers by indulging in exaggerated conducting, gesticulated
encouragement and face-pulling contortions. At the centre of
the joke, his conspiracy with the children, is the fact that the
parents can't see him and that he takes the risk that they
might. Thus he connects directly with the children and their
enjoyment – and, when they have finished singing, he resumes
his role as Master of Ceremonies.

Such an example reveals the skill of the headteacher but it
also tells us something about how he values children, how he
facilitates their enjoyment and how he seeks to use structured
school activities to maintain such values. It is a good indicator,
of the ethos of the school, for similar attitudes, with a mix of
warmth and structure, are to be found throughout. But how
might it feel to begin with?

Starting school

The first few days at school are likely to be particularly significant to children and to the attitudes which they form about
school learning. They are a milestone too, in that long road
towards independence from parents. Thus, for all parties, there
is a lot at stake. Most primary schools now take considerable
care over the induction of new children. A series of preliminary
visits to school is commonplace and the value of home visits
by teachers is also well established. A specially staggered
timetable is also often used in the first few weeks so that the
children enter in groups and can get used to their classroom
without being initially exposed to the full length of the school

day. However, such devices do not change the fundamentals of what is going on. Consider this account by a mother:

> Mary started school today – very excited about it – talking constantly about it. Only one tense moment when we arrived in class on the first day – mother an emotional wreck. Mary enjoyed her first day, but reluctant to tell me what she is doing, talks about Mrs Wilkinson being nice – also about helping Mrs White and the new ones tomorrow. Spent the rest of the afternoon watching television and talking about being a big girl at the school now.
>
> Slept all night in her *own* bed. Says now she is at school she needs to sleep all night in her own bed (from Barrett, 1986, p. 29).

Here we see both the anxiety and pain of the parting, on both sides, as the bond between mother and daughter changes its character. We see some of the teacher's strategies of involving Mary but also Mary's reluctance to talk about what she is doing. Perhaps she has not yet made sense of it herself. We see Mary's pride in 'being a big girl ... now' and her move towards independence.

The process of starting school thus brings anxiety and vulnerability, but it also promises growth and personal achievement for the child. If it goes well, then a new phase of life begins constructively and the child is likely to be well placed to accept the risks which are involved with future learning. If not, then self-confidence in school is likely to be much more difficult to establish.

With the first day or two over, there is still much to learn. The 'rules and routines' of classroom life are quite different from those of the home: 'Why should you put your hand up if you want to ask a question?', 'I could always go to the toilet without asking before', 'But I want to play outside now!', 'Why is it only two in the sand?', I think I'd like to go home now please'. The regulations of school take some getting used to and, for those young children who find them hard to recognize and apply, classroom life can seem to consist of a bewildering array of things one should not do. Yet teachers have little option but to work through establishing such conventions. For instance, the classic request of the infant school teacher, to 'sit

25

cross-legged with nice straight backs and don't fiddle with things', is very understandable when trying to provide high-quality storytelling to a large class of very young children.

Gradually, as the terms go on, children also have to learn and adjust to the curricular expectations of their teachers and of the National Curriculum. They have to learn how to 'do their maths work', what constitutes a satisfactory story and how to set about creative activities. The teacher may call them to account for any area of their work and children very soon learn that 'pleasing teacher' is a very good rule of thumb for getting through the day. This can be seen as a rational defensive strategy, for children are always in a relatively powerless position when it comes to the evaluation of school work. Unfortunately however, 'pleasing teacher' and pushing oneself to the limits of one's skill or understanding are not often the same thing. Thus, we have the common phenomenon of young children neither being fully stretched, nor stretching themselves, whilst over-burdened teachers struggle to keep up with the class as a whole. Indeed, whilst this is a problem all the way through primary school, a recent study of the first year of school, by Neville Bennett and Joy Kell, has shown the enormous difficulties of:

> delivering a ... curriculum in classes of sometimes wide age range, containing children with generally low levels of language and social skills and varied experiences of school, without adequate resources and assistance, whilst feeling under pressure from parents to achieve progress in the basics (Bennett and Kell, 1989, p. 25).

There are no easy answers to such problems, for our education system is designed and funded as a mass system with its roots in the old elementary schools of the last century. It is inevitable then, that the school lives of individual children must be structured by the necessities of organizing provision for relatively large numbers. Even so, there are choices to be made.

Structuring lives in school

The particular use of time, space and resources in a school is a matter of judgement and decision and the way the day is structured, the building used and resources deployed is thus likely to reflect particular philosophies and priorities. Whilst governors may have some influence on this, such matters are more normally the responsibility of the headteacher and his or her staff. There are three particularly important issues which need to be considered in structuring time, space and resources and they each derive from the paramount concern with schools as institutions of learning.

First, does the overall school provision facilitate an appropriate flow of opportunities for high quality learning situations – for an appropriate mix of listening, doing and discussing? Clearly responses to this question will depend to a great extent on the particular view of learning which is being adopted (see Chapter 1). If the emphasis is predominantly on 'listening' and more instructional, adult-directed learning then one would expect to find rooms set out for whole-class work and the regular use of class textbooks. Perhaps the school may even use a 'targeting' system in which children of similar attainments are taught together for some subjects. To implement the more individualized and active philosophy of Piaget's constructivism very varied resources are necessary. One would expect to find a large and wide-ranging library, writing resources and materials, direct access to artistic media such as paper, paint and clay, plenty of provision for different forms of play – bricks, construction kits, sand, water, home corners – and resources for a range of scientific, mathematical and technological investigations. In schools which adopt this philosophy, the school environment is often developed very richly, with ponds, nature and play areas outside and many colourful examples of children's work and eye-catching stimuli to their curiosity inside. The school is seen as a workshop of practical activity thus providing the direct experience through which children learn. Such provision would also be necessary if a more social constructivist approach to learning was adopted, but here, within the school day, one would expect a greater proportion of group work and more time spent in collective discussion of activities. Classroom layouts would reflect this, perhaps with a greater proportion of large tables for groups of children to work at and carpeted areas for discussion groups. Resources would reflect the approach too – for instance painting easels on which pairs of children could work, construction kits which are large enough for several children to use and design features such as bays and activity areas, which facilitate children talking to each other without disturbing other people.

A second question to ask about the structuring of time, space and resources concerns consistency. Are the policies and practices of the school internally consistent so that the child learner receives clear messages and is able to address learning challenges without organizational obstacles and distractions? It is not very helpful, for instance, for a school to adopt a constructivist philosophy of 'active learning', which suggests that each child will negotiate much of their programme of work, if the timetable fragments the school day so much that concentration on their activities is impossible. Nor is it much sense to encourage talk and group activity if the architecture of the school is such that other people will constantly be disturbed. Diverse and rich resources collected for individualized work are likely to go wasted if the class, in fact, tends to be organized on a whole-class basis. Similarly, children will get frustrated if, when they are encouraged to think for themselves, the resources to implement and extend their plans are not available.

The third major issue to be considered in the structuring of the school environment is a quantitative one. How much time is actually available during which children can learn? Wide variations can be created as different schools programme in their assemblies, dinner times and breaks, as they decide their administrative procedures for things like registration, dinner money, shoe changing and cloakroom use, and as they decide on their length of the school day. There is not much point, as a learner, in going to school if you spend a large proportion of the available time waiting for something to happen or for worthwhile opportunities to listen, do and discuss. Not, of course, that children would just wait in quite that way!

Children's culture and perspectives

Children do not just experience the routines, rules and structures of schools passively. They constantly act to get the most enjoyment from situations – they love 'to have a bit of fun', and 'to get a laugh'. Such occasions for laughter may be moments of relief in their relationships with the teacher-adults who have such power over them, and the significance of this is testified by the enduring popularity of comics such as the *Dandy* and the *Beano* with, in particular, the Bash Street Kids. Child culture belongs to children. Its very rationale is that it is developed as an antidote to adults. As any writer of children's fiction will tell you, the first thing one must do when writing a children's book is to get rid of the parents – then the adventures can really begin. In schools, these same concerns are manifest in the culture and activity of the playground, for 'playtime' and 'dinner-time play' provide opportunities for children to relate together with minimal adult supervision. Thus we see a whole panoply of games, rhymes, chants, dramas, fights and friendships which emerge in the playground. They change in character as children move up the school and they tend to be relatively gender specific – from 'Ring-a-ring-a-roses' to dance routines, and from 'Batman' to 'Power Rangers'. Some are individual, many others involve small groups of children whilst a few involve large numbers – a whole playground full of children somewhat unkindly imitating the gait of the supervising teacher is a vivid memory from my own childhood.

It has been suggested that children's games and activities enable them to develop social conventions and to begin to experience some of the complexities of social relationships which they will come across in later life. It is certainly the case that playground culture develops with codes of appropriate behaviour and of fairness, with procedures for conflict resolution, with complex and multiple friendship patterns, with orders of status and with the use of power – particularly by boys in the ways in which they tend to dominate the space through their games. Perhaps it is not so much unlike adult life?

Each child must, of course, cope with the culture of the school as they find it, and for some, this can be hard. To broaden this point, we have to relate each child's position as a learner to the social context which the children's social world provides. Indeed, there is evidence that levels of academic achievements and the nature of each child's relationship with teachers, do have an influence on the ways in which they are treated by other children. Thus, if some children are relatively unsuccessful at school work or feel undervalued by their teachers, they may find it more difficult to establish close relationships with more successful peers. Children in such positions then tend to join together and provide a type of mutual support for each other. By the junior years such groups may form into 'gangs' and start to develop relatively anti-school perspectives. A similar process with the more 'successful' children is likely to have opposite and more positive results – but then we have the beginnings of the polarized groups of children which are a notable feature of many secondary schools.

Child culture thus has considerable influence over children. It provides cultural resources and sources of solidarity which enable many children to cope with the demands made by adults. In turn though, it imposes demands of its own – to be wearing the right sort of shoes, to watch the right programmes, to collect the right toys, to speak 'properly'. Child culture at school is thus also something which children very much have to cope with. For most children it will strengthen their sense of identity and worth and thus enable them to engage in learning tasks with the secure confidence that their peers will not think badly of them if something goes wrong. For a few others, the world of the playground can be as trying as that of the classroom particularly if teasing or bullying emerge. Where self-esteem is vulnerable in such settings, then some help is urgently required.

Diversity in school experience

For much of this chapter, I have written about 'children' without distinguishing a great deal between the various groups. And yet, pupil experience of school life does vary considerably.

For instance, for girls and for boys, such differences are likely to be manifested through child culture and teacher expectations, and they may result in the boys and girls having quite different feelings about school, influences on identity and learning outcomes. Children's interpretation of school life will also vary in relation to their different cultural or ethnic backgrounds and in respect of the ways in which these factors affect how people at school interact with them. In economic terms, modern British society became more unequal during the 1980s and early 1990s, with increasing disparities in wealth and the families of some children facing considerable poverty and insecurity. It also continued to become more culturally diverse with British ethnic minorities both asserting and having to defend their identities. For instance, for children of some British Asian families their bilingualism and religious beliefs have not always been fully recognized in national education legislation or in school practices. Indeed, discriminatory attitudes affecting both social class and 'ethnicity' can produce problems for young children in schools, as in any other setting.

Additionally, there are the diverse experiences of children who have special educational needs, whether of a physical sort or concerning learning or behavioural difficulties. Almost a fifth of children may be deemed to have some form of special need at some point in their schooling and most will be taught in mainstream schools. In 1993, for instance, only 1.3 per cent of children in England were being educated in special schools.

The diversity in the experiences of children is very great and, although we must consider the primary education or school systems as a whole, we must not lose sight of the particular needs of groups or of individuals.

Conclusion

Experiencing primary school presents many new challenges to young children. It is a distinct stage on their progress towards adulthood but many new situations, demands and types of relationship have to be encountered and overcome. It is a tribute to the caring approach of most primary schools that children are normally very happy and that the years of primary education are so often seen so positively in retrospect.

Suggestions for further reading

For an overview of the way children interact with their teachers and each other in primary schools, see:

Pollard, A. (1985) *The Social World of the Primary School*. London: Cassell.

Two books which manage to convey much of children's experience of starting school are:

Jackson, B. (1979) *Starting School*. London: Croom Helm.

Barrett, G. (1986) *Starting School, An Evaluation of the Experience*. London: AMMA.

Jackson's book is particularly good for its case studies of children of different cultures.

For expert advice on what high quality education for young children should be like see:

Early Years Curricular Group (1989) *Early Childhood Education*. Stoke-on-Trent: Trentham.

More general books on children's perspectives on school experiences are:

Goodnow, J. and Burns, A, (1985) *Home and School, A Child's-Eye View*. London: Allen and Unwin.

Slukin, A. (1981) *Growing Up in the Playground*. London: Croom Helm.

Davies, B. (1982) *Life in the Classroom and Playground*. London: Routledge.

For a book which tracks case-study 'pupil careers' as children develop through the whole seven years of their primary school, see:

Pollard, A. and Filer, A. (1996) *The Social World of Pupil Careers*. London: Cassell.

Chapter 3

CURRICULUM, ASSESSMENT AND LEARNING

We begin this important chapter with some basic principles which link curriculum and learning.

Some things which we should not forget

The first point to be made about the curriculum of primary schools is that, whilst the subject-matter to be studied is very important, the curriculum cannot be just about factual knowledge. Children in primary schools are young. They are developing physically, emotionally and socially as well as intellectually. They learn best, as we have seen, through their active engagement in an ever-widening range of experiences and with the support and involvement of both adults and peers. What they learn in school is often complex and it may sometimes be a little unpredictable. Children will filter and interpret what they are taught as they struggle to make sense of it, so that we cannot assume that what children learn is a direct reflection of the curriculum which is presented to them.

One helpful and perceptive way in which the primary school curriculum has been conceptualized by Alan Blyth (1984) is as a process in which children's development, their experiences and the curriculum which is offered to them intertwine. More specifically, the curriculum is seen as 'a planned intervention' between children's development and their experience. It is thus something which adults control and for which we have to accept responsibility. A simplified representation of Blyth's model is shown in Figure 3.1.

The strength of this model is that it provides a sense of perspective. It makes it clear that the process of learning will go on, in some way, irrespective of any particular form of the curriculum. It thus lays responsibility for the 'planned

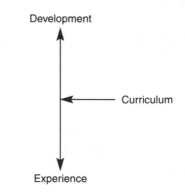

Development

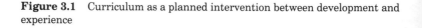

Curriculum

Experience

Figure 3.1 Curriculum as a planned intervention between development and experience

interventions of the curriculum' squarely at the door of adults. Of course, this then raises issues to do with values and beliefs. What should children learn? What will be our future needs as a society? What are the needs of our children?

Alan Blyth faces such issues directly by identifying the purpose of education as being to 'enable' – to make it possible for children to fulfil their personal potential, to understand their society and to exercise choices within it democratically. It is helpful to keep such basic principles in mind, since some of the fundamental issues involved in curriculum design were somewhat obscured in the political and professional debates that were associated with the introduction of the National Curriculum and assessment procedures.

Clearly, to provide any curriculum is a considerable challenge. We now look at some of the ways in which teachers may set about meeting it.

Planning a curriculum

One effective way of thinking about curriculum, following the advice of Her Majesty's Inspectorate (HMI) in 1985, is to consider four key elements – knowledge, skills, concepts and attitudes. Teachers thus try to:

- extend children's *knowledge* in their area of study;
- develop *skills* which enable children to control and direct their own learning, including social, linguistic, scientific, mathematical and manipulative skills;
- build *concepts* which enable children to organize, generalize, and relate ideas and thus form a basis for analysis and for making informed judgements;
- develop positive *attitudes* in the children towards both learning and each other. For instance, to question, to listen, to observe, to concentrate when learning. To respect each other and the cultures which make up our society, to work both individually and co-operatively with others.

Such a framework is a great help in thinking analytically about the curriculum but it is, essentially, content-free. A question remains then: what should the content of the curriculum be?

That the curriculum should be directly rooted in children's interests is a point of view which is of great historical significance in primary education. It reflects the influence of two educational reports, the Hadow Report of 1931 (Board of Education, 1931) and the Plowden Report of 1967 (CACE, 1967), and teachers' accumulated experience of working with young children particularly in the 1960s and 1970s. Over the years, many ways of working through children's interests were developed, including the 'negotiated curriculum'. For instance, in an example from 1988, just before the introduction of the National Curriculum framework in England, a teacher of a class of 6- and 7- year-olds in a Bristol primary school suggested to her class that they might take the theme of 'weather' as their topic for the term. Some ideas related to weather were discussed and each child then spent some time producing a record of what, in their view, would be interesting and worthwhile aspects of the topic to cover. Some examples of the children's work are provided in Figures 3.2 and 3.3.

The teacher then asked the children to share their ideas in groups and then, a little later, each group offered their thoughts back to the whole class. Following this, representatives of each group drew up a basic structure for a whole-class 'web

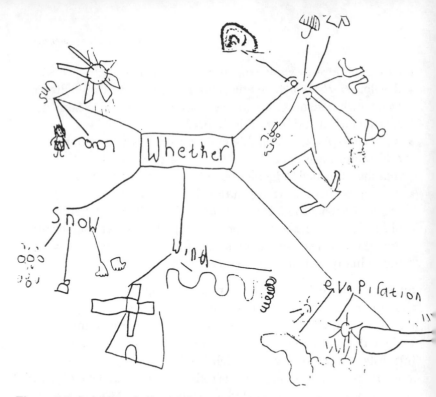

Figure 3.2 A child's web diagram for a topic on the weather

Figure 3.3 Another child's web diagram for a topic on the weather

diagram' to provide a visual representation of the thinking and planning which had gone on. Each group then came and entered their ideas on to the web. The result is reproduced in Figure 3.4.

It is worth noting here how more refined the children's ideas had become. There was now a greater degree of hierarchy and organization in their thinking about weather (sun, clothing, seasons, etc.) and they had identified both chains of linked ideas and places where options exist. The negotiation and planning process was itself an educational experience and the children's web diagram was displayed in the classroom throughout the term as a constant reference point.

The class teacher took the children's ideas and used them to construct a web diagram for her own planning (see Figure 3.5). In this case she used a pro forma designed by the school to ensure that the children were exposed to an appropriate range of subject content in each topic which they covered, as determined by the school's curriculum policies. This chart was then communicated to the children's parents so that they could support their children through the term and was also used as an ongoing planning tool for the planning and preparation of each week. The progressive exploration of the ideas contained in the web diagrams lasted all term. The children worked with a wide range of media and were also taken on an educational visit to a weather station to stimulate their thinking and to give them direct experience of an aspect of the topic. At the end of term copies of the teacher's web diagram were used to provide a record of the work of each individual child by highlighting which parts of the topic each child had participated in. This record was made available to the next teacher and to parents by being placed in the portfolio of each child's work.

This is an exciting, immediate and flexible way of planning a programme of work for a class, and has been used as the basic planning tool of 'child-centred' approaches to curriculum provision for a great many years. It has particular strengths in terms of the 'relevance' of the focus of study to the children and in terms of the 'coherence' in their learning experience which can be achieved.

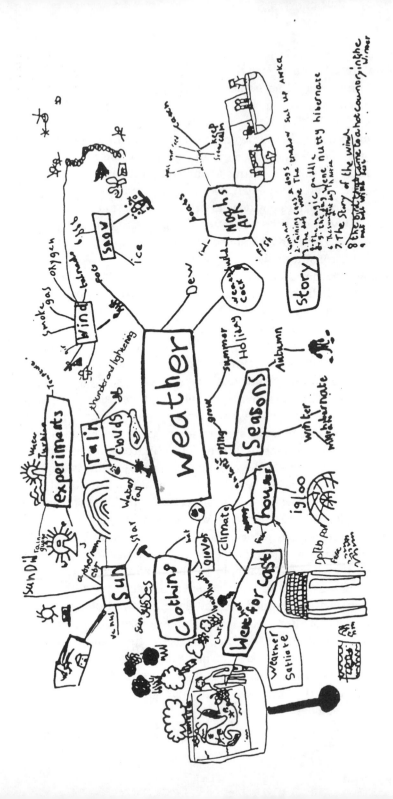

Figure 3.4 A whole-class web diagram on the weather

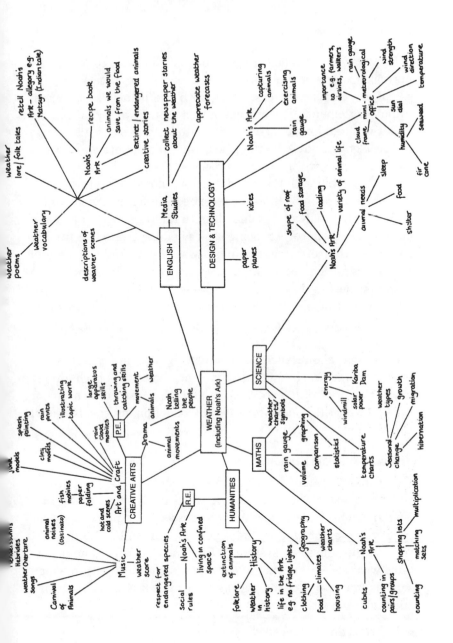

WEATHER (including Noah's Ark)

ENGLISH
- Media Studies
- Noah's Ark
  - recipe book
  - animals we would save from the flood
  - extinct/endangered animals
  - creative stories
- weather lore/folk tales
- retell Noah's Ark – allegory e.g. Matsyu (Indian tale)
- weather poems
- weather vocabulary
- descriptions of weather scenes
- collect newspaper stories about the weather
- appreciate weather forecasts

DESIGN & TECHNOLOGY
- kites
- paper planes
- Noah's Ark
  - capturing animals
  - exercising animals
  - rain gauge
- Noah's Ark
  - shape of roof
  - food storage
  - loading
  - variety of animal life
  - animal needs
    - sleep
    - food
    - shelter
- mini-meteorological office
  - importance to e.g. farmers, airlines, walkers
  - rain gauge
  - wind strength
  - wind direction
  - temperature
  - sun dial
  - humidity
  - seaweed
  - fir cone
  - cloud frame

CREATIVE ARTS
- Art and Craft
  - junk models
  - splash painting
  - rain prints
  - illustrating topic work
  - rain cloud mobiles
  - clay models
  - fish mobiles
  - paper folding
  - hot and cold scenes
- Drama
  - animal movements
  - Noah telling the people
  - animals
  - weather
  - movement
- P.E.
  - throwing and catching skills
  - large apparatus skills
- Music
  - Hebrides
  - Mendelssohn's
  - weather Overture
  - animal noises (ostinato)
  - Carnival of Animals
  - songs
  - weather score
  - respect for endangered species

HUMANITIES
- R.E.
  - Noah's Ark
    - living in confined space
    - extinction of animals
    - Social rules
- History
  - folklore
  - weather in history
  - life in the Ark e.g. no fridge, lights
- Geography
  - clothing
  - food
  - climates
  - housing
  - weather charts

SCIENCE
- weather charts/symbols
- energy
  - Kariba Dam
  - solar power
  - windmill
- temperature charts
- weather types
- Seasonal change
- growth
- migration
- hibernation

MATHS
- rain gauge
- volume
- graphing
- comparison
- statistics
- Noah's Ark
  - cubits
  - counting in pairs/groups
  - Shopping lists
  - multiplication
  - matching sets
  - counting

However, as applied in schools across the country, the approach was also the subject of some severe criticisms. One set of criticisms were associated with the principle of 'curriculum entitlement'. The argument was that, if we take it that all children should have an equal right to learn a particular range of knowledge and skills then how can judgements about what to study be left to the uncertainties of teachers simply talking and negotiating with their pupils up and down the country?

A second area of criticism concerned the 'progression' which children experience from one class to another. What degree of cumulation is there? Are some topics being repeated? A further issue was that of 'breadth'. What was the overall coverage of the topics which the children experienced? Were some issues being neglected in successive classes? Were areas such as science, technology or the creative arts being satisfactorily addressed? Was too much energy going into reading, writing and maths?

Thinking about such issues highlighted many areas for improvement in the continuity and breadth of children's curricular learning experiences and this provided a major plank in the rationale for the introduction of the National Curriculum.

The National Curriculum

Following the Education Reform Act 1988, the early 1990s saw the progressive introduction of a national curriculum into England and Wales together with associated procedures for pupil assessment and for the reporting of results. For the first time in the education system of England and Wales, curricular aims were set out as part of the legal framework within which schools must act. As the legislation expressed it, each school's curriculum must:

- be broad and balanced;
- promote the spiritual, moral, cultural, mental and physical development of pupils at school and of society;
- prepare pupils for the opportunities, responsibilities and experiences of adult life.

More specifically, the orders of the National Curriculum set out the particular subject content to be taught and requirements for pupil assessment and for the reporting of results were also established. The rationale for this degree of specification and central direction by the Secretary of State for Education was that education had previously been controlled by the 'producers' (teachers) and now had to be made more responsive to 'consumers' (parents and industry).

The Education Reform Act was the most significant legislation since the 1944 Education Act and many teachers recognized that it was based on very different values. For instance, here are the comments of one headteacher who found the changes difficult to accept:

> The 1944 Education Act was about equality of opportunity ... It led to the comprehensive dream which sought to honour each individual's potential ... We tried to make education a fruitful experience, building self-respect and self-knowledge ... The ethos was co-operative, not competitive. It also had a social purpose, which was to heal the divisions in society.
>
> The 1988 Education Reform Act was all about inequality and its mainspring was coercion. It ... turned all the values upside down. It stopped trusting teachers and pupils. Choice was ruled out. Education ceased to be an exploration of the wonders of the world ... and became an exploration of what pupils couldn't understand and an insistence that it mattered.
>
> National testing is more about highlighting failure than building on success. It is also about competition, not just between pupils but between teachers and schools, hence the league tables. However, at least it has a clear purpose, based on a credible belief that the world is an economic jungle and that children should learn to adapt to its laws (Bob Spooner, retired headteacher, writing in *Education*, 28 January 1994).

In considering the National Curriculum and assessment then, it is clear that we are dealing with terrain about which very strong feelings have existed. Indeed, there was a reciprocal mistrust between politicians and teachers through much of the 1980s and early 1990s as radically new national policies were enacted.

Nevertheless, a National Curriculum for England and Wales was implemented, and the principle of having a national curriculum framework was gradually accepted by a majority of teachers. However, the initial content and procedures introduced by the government were found to be over-complex, difficult to implement and, in the view of some, harmful to the quality of children's school experience. Such concerns contributed to a great deal of public debate about education in the early 1990s. In 1993, the two separate national bodies which the government had set up, for curriculum (NCC) and assessment (SEAC), were merged to become the School Curriculum and Assessment Authority (SCAA). In December 1993, the Chairman of SCAA, Sir Ron Dearing, reported that the National Curriculum and assessment procedures needed an immediate and fundamental review. This was achieved in a new spirit of consultation with teachers and a 'slimmed down' National Curriculum was created and was adopted from the 1995–96 school year. There were parallel development in Wales, led by the Awdurdod Cwricwlwm ac Asesu Cymru (ACAC).

The revised National Curriculum, like its predecessor, uses 'subjects', 'programmes of study' and 'attainment targets' as basic building blocks. From these, a framework to guide curriculum and assessment practices in schools has been constructed. Within that framework, teachers have the scope, working through school policies, to interpret the precise ways in which the curriculum in presented to the children. Indicative proportions of time to be spent on each subject have been offered, but, in primary schools, 20 per cent of the time available for teaching and learning is supposed to be available to be used at teachers' discretion.

The subjects which provide the basic National Curriculum framework for England are fairly traditional and are set out in Table 3.1.

In Wales, the Cymraeg provides for pupils to be given 'opportunities to develop and apply their knowledge and understanding of the cultural, economic, environmental and linguistic characteristics of Wales' and this is encouraged in work across all curriculum subjects. Although the curriculum closely resembles that in England, specific national curriculum documents for art, music, geography and history and Welsh are provided by ACAC for Welsh schools. There are particular requirements regarding when Welsh must be taught and these are summarized in Table 3.2.

Table 3.1   The core and other foundation subjects of the National Curriculum

Core foundation subjects	Other foundation subjects
English	History
Mathematics	Geography
Science	Design and technology
	Information technology
	Music
	Art
	PE

Every school must also make provision for Religious education

Table 3.2   National Curriculum requirements for the teaching of Welsh and English in Wales

	At Key Stage 1	At Key Stage 2
In schools where Welsh *is* the main medium of instruction	Welsh is a core foundation subject. English is another foundation subject.	Welsh and English are both core foundation subjects.
In schools where Welsh *is not* the main medium of instruction	English is a core foundation subject. Welsh is another foundation subject.	English is a core foundation subject. Welsh is another foundation subject.

The 'core subjects' are expected to take up the 'majority of classroom time' in primary schools and, indeed, research in England shows that approximately 35 per cent of time on English, 15 per cent on maths and 8 per cent on science is not uncommon, with rather smaller proportions of time being spent on other subjects. Schools must also provide religious education, though parents have particular rights to withdraw their child if they do not endorse the form this may take.

'Programmes of study' are rather like a conventional syllabus and set out what children should know, be able to do and to understand at the end of the course of teaching. For each subject there are 'general requirements' and these are elaborated with more specific statements of what should be taught for each aspect of the subject. For instance, the first general requirement for English is illustrated in Figure 3.6.

English should develop pupils' abilities to communicate effectively in speech and writing and to listen with understanding. It should also enable them to be enthusiastic, responsive and knowledgeable readers.

a To develop effective *speaking and listening* pupils should be taught to:
- use the vocabulary and grammar of standard English;
- formulate, clarify and express their ideas;
- adapt their speech to a widening range of circumstances and demands;
- listen, understand and respond appropriately to others.

b To develop as effective *readers*, pupils should be taught to:
- read accurately, fluently and with understanding;
- understand and respond to the texts they read;
- read, analyse and evaluate a wide range of texts, including literature from the English literary heritage and from other cultures and traditions.

c To develop as effective *writers*, pupils should be taught to use:
- compositional skills – developing ideas and communicating meaning to a reader, using a wide-ranging vocabulary and an effective style, organising and structuring sentences grammatically and whole texts coherently;
- presentational skills – accurate punctuation, correct spelling and legible handwriting;
- a widening variety of forms for different purposes.

Figure 3.6 The first general requirement for English in the 1995 version of the National Curriculum of England and Wales

In some subjects, there are major subdivisions within the programme of study and, for assessment purposes, these are associated with particular 'attainment targets'. For instance, those for English are italicized in Figure 3.6 – speaking and listening, reading and writing. Table 3.3 provides a summary of *all* the attainment targets of the National Curriculum subjects which apply to primary schools. For a synopsis of the actual content of each subject, see Chapter 9.

The thinking behind the National Curriculum is that the specification of the content to be studied will ensure adequate coverage of basic, core subjects whilst also providing for breadth. The programmes of study, which run throughout the years of compulsory schooling from age 5 to 16, are intended to ensure progression from year to year and to provide continuity between schools. Specific attainment targets are intended to set clear goals and to provide a basis for pupil assessment at the ages of 7, 11 and 14. These ages are the endpoints of what are known as 'Key Stages 1, 2 and 3'.

In reviewing the evidence on the impact of the National Curriculum (HMCI 1995, Pollard *et al.*, 1994), there seems little doubt that it has overcome many of the weaknesses of what was previously, for all its richness, a relatively uncoordinated topic-by-topic form of practice. However, the version introduced in the first five years did produce very serious problems and wise and constructive parents, governors and teachers must continue to watch cautiously and act responsively as it is implemented and developed in its revised form.

Among the questions which might be raised are the following:

- How relevant and meaningful to the children is the curriculum which they experience; and, what is the quality of their engagement with each subject?
- How does the specification of the curriculum in detail affect the creativity and imagination of teachers and children? Does it broaden or constrain the range of their knowledge and the development of their skills?
- Is the curriculum content appropriate and who controls it? For instance, when the National Curriculum was revised there

Table 3.3 Attainment targets within each National Curriculum subject as they apply to primary education in England and Wales

Subject	Attainment Targets in England	Attainment Targets in Wales
English	Speaking and Listening Reading Writing	Speaking and Listening Reading Writing
Welsh	Not applicable	Oral (speaking, listening and viewing) Reading Writing
Maths	Using and applying mathematics Number Shape, space and measures (and handling data in Key Stage 2 only)	Using and applying mathematics Number Shape, space and measures (and handling data in Key Stage 2 only)
Science	Experimental and investigative science Life processes and living things Materials and their properties Physical processes	Experimental and investigative science Life processes and living things Materials and their properties Physical processes
Design and technology	Designing Making	Designing Making
Information technology	Information technology capability	Information technology capability
History	History	History
Geography	Geography	Geography
Art	Investigating and making Knowledge and understanding	Understanding Making Investigating
Music	Performing and composing Listening and appraising	Performing Composing Appraising
Physical Education	Physical education	Physical education

was a great deal of debate about the selective interpretation of history and about the appropriateness of the emphasis on Standard English for our culturally diverse societies.

- How does the National Curriculum framework allow for innovation and development within schools?
- How does the National Curriculum affect curriculum planning? Does it imply a need for linear, subject-based programmes of study or can cross-subject themes and projects be used?

This last question is of particular significance to the focus of this book on learning, for a crude interpretation of the structure of the National Curriculum could mean that the agenda for children's learning would be set by the national documentation alone. If that were so, the underlying psychological model could tend towards the one I have termed 'behaviourist', in which adult-determined knowledge would to be passed to the passive child (see Chapter 1). In fact, teachers have shown great commitment and skill in implementing the curriculum so that constructivist models of learning have been used to ensure that children retain opportunities to identify with and become actively involved with their work. There is considerable evidence that primary school teachers are very committed to attempts to make the curriculum as meaningful as possible to their pupils.

Indeed, in the midst of all the discussions about curriculum which take place between adults, we should remember the children directly. In particular, we need to consider how they may respond to our curriculum – that 'planned intervention' between their development and their experience. My own experience suggests that they are very likely to think about the curriculum in ways which are quite different from those of adults. Never mind programmes of study and attainment targets, is it 'boring' or 'interesting'? Does it involve writing? Can we talk to each other and *do* things? For instance, here are comments of some 6-year-olds:

> Construction is my favourite. Once I got to play there all morning one day – no one noticed. It was good.

Maths is very good because when you do the colouring you just write in your book.

I like writing 'cos it helps you learn more words and to get your words neat and small.

I don't really like writing, 'cos your arms ache if you do two pages or more. I like doing the picture but the writing ... I don't really like doing it.

I like reading the best 'cos I don't waste time with chatting.

I don't like reading 'cos it takes hours to get to your turn but in the end I like it 'cos Miss gets funny.

Writing is boring and sometimes I start and think, and get day-dreams, and its dinner time, and then its boring again ... because you have to keep it neat and because you have to keep on thinking of words and no one tells you and it goes on and on.

Well, we do these maths cards and some are fun and some aren't, ... and you try to get on to different stages. I'm on Stage 8.

Why not ask some of the children at your school what they think of the things they do? The curriculum as it is directly experienced and thought about by children is usually in terms of the nature of the activity, the degree of autonomy which it offers and even the status which this gives them. For young children especially, thoughts about particular subjects seem to be hard to disentangle from thoughts about the classroom experience which they actually produce.

The initial introduction of the National Curriculum was likened to a 'massive experiment' and, as we have seen, the early results were a rather mixed bag. In its revised form the National Curriculum has been constructed following consultation with parents, teachers and others and it promises a great deal. However, we must continue to look for evidence about its effects. A first test of whether it is all worthwhile will arguably be found in children's thoughts and feelings. This can then be combined with information on educational achievements and with an assessment of the extent to which education is contributing to politically defined economic and social needs and to the quality of life.

Assessing Learning

In recent years, the assessment of children's learning has probably engendered even more controversy than the debates on curriculum. One of the reasons for this is that assessment may seem a rather 'hard' procedure to apply to young children at formative stages in their development. In addition, assessment is a complicated and technical process and it is very easy for people to debate it at cross purposes. Most fundamentally though, there are very different views on the uses to which assessment information should be put.

There are two main reasons for assessing children's learning. The first concerns the teaching-learning process itself and involves collecting assessment evidence so that children's problems can be diagnosed and so that new learning tasks can be pitched at an appropriate level of challenge. Regular assessment conducted for this purpose is known as 'formative assessment'. A second sound reason for assessing is to provide a means of taking stock of a situation at the end of a period of learning. Such information may be used for future planning or it could be used for reporting on progress that has been made, for instance, to the children themselves and parents or, in aggregated forms, to governors or the Local Education Authority. This is called 'summative assessment'.

The assessment procedures which are associated with the National Curriculum provide for both formative and summative assessment and are structured by the 'attainment targets' for each curriculum subject and by 'levels'. For the core curriculum in England and Wales each child's level of achievement for each attainment target is measured on an eight-point scale. This covers the expected range of development between ages 5 and 14 years (see Figure 3.7).

We can now look at each form of assessment in turn.

Formative assessment

Teachers, with the advice of Local Education Authorities, have considerable control over formative assessment and the process is continuous throughout each child's life in school. The precise

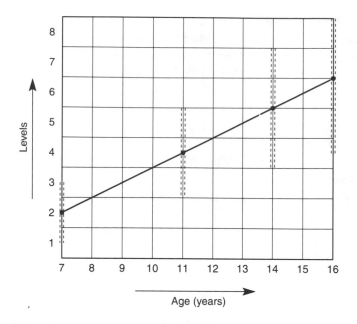

Figure 3.7 Sequence of pupil achievement of levels between ages 5 and 14 (Prior to the 1995 review this was a ten-point scale also embracing 14- to 16-year-olds

form which such teacher assessment (TA) takes may vary depending on the approach to learning which is adopted in each school and classroom. After all, any evidence collected or judgements made must feed directly back to improve the teaching which is then offered to the children.

Teachers have always engaged in formative assessment in one way or another but this had tended to happen on an *ad hoc* basis. Indeed, before the Education Reform Act, formal recording of such assessment was often minimal. At the same time though, there has been a mounting body of research evidence showing that teachers acquire a very great deal of sophisticated knowledge about children as they work with them, even though much of this is tacit and unrecorded. It may well be the case that such tacit knowledge feeds the intuitive, creative and empathic aspects of teaching – aspects which make the job fulfilling and give it a personal, human dimension. However, intuition can also lead to distortions in perception if it is unsupported by more objective checks and balances.

Teachers tackled these issues with great commitment in the early 1990s because they could see how their efforts would benefit the children directly. They collected evidence on which to base their judgements and they engaged in 'moderation' meetings with other teachers to evolve shared interpretations. This had very positive results and there is evidence that collecting and recording data for formative assessment helps teachers to avoid over-simple categorizations of children, to improve diagnostic skills and to raise expectations about children's potential.

Whilst the benefits of formative teacher assessment are considerable, there are also difficulties. The most obvious is that busy teachers simply have very little available time to carry out the type of careful, evidence-based assessment procedures which are, ideally, necessary. Following the experience of the early 1990s, this led to a reduction in the requirements made of teachers in England and Wales for this form of assessment. For instance, from 1994, teacher assessment was only required for the core subjects in primary schools, though this is subject to review. A further development to ease the assessment burden was the introduction of 'level descriptions'. These are descriptions, for each attainment target, of what a teacher might characteristically expect a pupil to know and be able to do or understand if he or she is to be assessed as attaining that level. The required teacher judgement is of what level description is the 'best fit' with the child's performance. For instance, within the subject of English, the attainment target for 'reading' has the level descriptions as shown in Figure 3.8. These are expected to be appropriate for most children of primary school age.

Teachers' efforts to develop their formative assessment skills helped to develop their professional expertise as well as benefiting the children. These achievements were recognized in the Dearing Report and the advantage of 'going with the grain of teacher professionalism' (Mrs Shephard, Secretary of State for Education, 1994) was reflected in the introduction of level

Level 1:   Pupils recognise familiar words in simple texts. They use their knowledge of letters and sound-symbol relationships in order to read words and to establish meaning when reading aloud. In these activities they sometimes require support. They express their responses to poems, stories and non-fiction by identifying aspects they like.

Level 2:   Pupils' reading of simple texts shows understanding and is generally accurate. They express opinions about major events or ideas in stories, poems and non-fiction. The use more than one strategy, such as phonic, graphic, syntactic and contextual, in reading unfamiliar words and establishing meaning.

Level 3:   Pupils read a range of texts fluently and accurately. They read independently, using strategies appropriately to establish meaning. In responding to fiction and non-fiction they show understanding of the main points and express preferences. They use their knowledge of the alphabet to locate books and find information.

Level 4:   In responding to a range of texts, pupils show understanding of significant ideas, themes, events and characters, beginning to use inference and deduction. They refer to the text when explaining their views. They locate and use ideas and information.

Figure 3.8   Level descriptions for the reading attainment target of the 1995 National Curriculum for England and Wales

descriptions and the endorsement of teacher judgement which they represent.

When reporting to parents, the outcomes of formative, teacher assessment are given parity in importance alongside more summative and standardized assessment results.

Summative assessment

Summative assessment, as part of the Education Reform Act 1988, can primarily be seen as a means of measuring and reporting pupils' levels of achievement. Such reporting is required at the end of each key stage and thus pupils take national standardized assessment tests (SATs) at the ages of 7, 11 and 14. GCSEs are taken at the age of 16.

In the early 1990s, when the tests were introduced for 7-year-olds, there was considerable opposition from parents and teachers. Indeed some teachers refused to carry out the assessments because they felt that that they would distort the curriculum, cause pupil anxiety, be very difficult to manage and not reveal anything new. There were also objections to the use of the results from pupils in particular schools being used to construct crude 'league tables' of schools. In the summer of 1993 there was a complete boycott of testing when primary school teachers were joined by secondary teachers who also rejected the tests for 14-year-olds. Even after some lightening of the assessment requirements, only 52 per cent of primary schools reported results for 7-year-olds in 1994. By 1995 SATs were refined again and were implemented by most schools, though still with some significant professional reluctance.

When pupils are required to carry out a SAT their performance is judged against nationally set criteria and levels. In this way, each child's level of achievement can be gauged. The following are examples of standard assessment tests as used in 1995.

English: spelling

At the end of Key Stage 1, children whose spelling had been assessed at 'Level 2' or above by their teachers were given a special standardized test. This was administered to individuals, groups or whole classes using copies of a specially printed booklet, 'The Bike Race', which were completed by each child.

In the first part of the test, 12 simple pictures were presented to the children and the teacher gave instructions guided by a recommended script. For instance:

> Let's look at the ninth picture (the bread). What is it a picture of? It is some bread. Write in the missing letters of 'bread'. If you wish to change your answer, you can cross it out or rub it out.

Figure 3.9 Detailed illustration of SAT for spelling at Key Stage 1

In the second part of the test, the children began by listening to the teacher reading the story of 'The Bike Race'. The teacher then read the story again whilst the children read it in their booklets, but they were also asked to fill in 20 words which were missing from the text:

> I am going to read the story again. When you come to a space, wait for me to tell you the word and then write it in the space. If you are not sure how to spell the word, just have a go and write in the letters which you think look right.
>
> It is a ____ (hot) sunny day. The race is ____ (about) to begin. Paul ____ (pushes) down hard on his handlebars. Today he is going to win. Today he has to prove ____ (himself) to the cycling ____ (group).

Altogether, 32 marks were awarded for the two tests. 'Levels' for spelling were then given as follows:

Less than 7 marks	Level 2 not awarded
7–10 marks	Level 2C awarded
11–14 marks	Level 2B awarded
15–19 marks	Level 2A awarded
20–32 marks	Level 3 awarded

Mathematics: number

A 'four in a line' activity contributed to the assessment of pupils' attainment at mathematics at the end of Key Stage 2. Although it was a test of whether the child 'knows and can use number facts, including addition and subtraction' at attainment Level 2, it was presented as a game for a group of four children. The teacher gave each child a 'four in a line' sheet, as illustrated in Figure 3.10.

The children were then each issued with a set of ten sequenced cards, each requiring a calculation which they could attempt using apparatus if they wished. One set, for instance, posed the sums indicated in Figure 3.11.

The children completed each round of calculation as a group and, where their answer was on their 'four in a line' sheet, they crossed it out. As the sequence of ten calculations was completed, the children were encouraged to see how many horizontal, vertical or diagonal lines they could make from having four crossings-out. In modelling a television game show, this created some interest but the outcome was not part of the assessment scoring. For this, teachers recorded one mark for each child for each of their correct answers and these were used, together with marks from two other activities, to indicate whether or not each child had achieved 'Level 2' in mathematics.

There are all sorts of potential difficulties in carrying out such tests. For instance, it is by no means clear that a test can be carried out under standard conditions in school situations. Classrooms and teachers vary. Can SATs therefore be fair? Second, there are problems over what a standard assessment test can attempt to measure. Will what they can measure be of any real educational significance? Third, to what extent should all children carry out the same tasks or should the teacher be trusted to present tests which are specifically appropriate? Fourth, how much time and cost is taken up by the assessment process, and is it all worthwhile?

The SAT and Teacher Assessment results have equal status and are reported to the parents of each child aged 7 and 11. No results at this individual level will be published more widely.

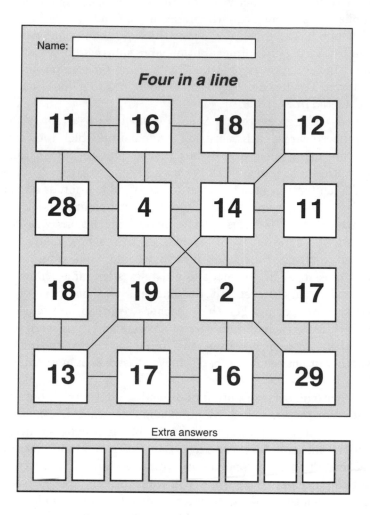

Figure 3.10 A 'four in a line' sheet used for the assessment of pupil attainment at number, Level 2, 1995

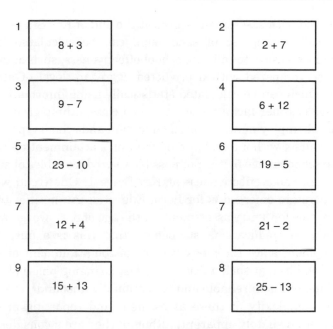

Figure 3.11 Number calculations set for pupils being assessed in number at Level 2 using a 'four in a line' sheet

However, it has been proposed that aggregated results for each school should be published in the form of 'league tables'. This reflects a government belief, in the inimitable words of John Patten, who was once Secretary of State for Education, that 'performance tables help to drive up standards' and 'the cat's out of the bag and there's no way pussy can be put back in again' (June 1994). Two main forms of league table have been developed. First, tables of 'raw' data are made up from the actual attainment scores of pupils which are aggregated for each school. They thus reflect absolute levels of achievement in each school, but they indicate nothing about whether the score of each school is 'good', 'bad' or 'indifferent' considering its circumstances and the needs of its pupils. For this, tables which show 'added value' are suggested. Added value is a measure of the gain which has been made by pupils whilst they have been in a school and have grown from, say age 7 to age 11. Thus assessment scores at the end of Key Stage 1 can be compared with assessment scores at the end of Key Stage 2 and the relative progress of each pupil can be calculated. In a further extension to indicate school effectiveness, such data can then be compared with a predicted aggregate level of attainment which can be calculated statistically using information on a range of other factors, such as social class, ethnic group, sex, parental employment, parental education and school type.

Of course, without evidence of children's attainment on entry to the school at age 5, it is not possible to produce tables of added value or school effectiveness at Key Stage 1. One trend which has therefore emerged is for Local Education Authorities to set up systems for 'entry assessment' at the age of 5. However, many teachers and educationalists believe that this is a misguided development since the measurement of the attainment of such young children at such a fragile but fast changing phase of their development is unreliable and educationally unsound.

The complexity of these assessment and reporting procedures is immediately apparent, although they are a considerable simplification over the pre-1995 requirements. They are likely to continue to be a challenge to those who have to make the system work in practice, and teacher concern about league tables and entry assessment is likely to remain strong.

There are also several dangers here in respect of the principles of the 'enabling curriculum' with which we began this chapter. First, whilst 'high stakes' testing goes on there will continue to be a temptation for teachers and schools to tailor their curriculum to match those things which are to be tested – so that published 'results' are seen to be good. Ironically, given the aims of the Education Reform Act, this could have serious consequences for the breadth of curriculum covered which could remain relatively narrowly focused on basic skills. Second, there is the question of the effects which testing and the reporting of results have on such young children. Will those who do less well develop a sense of failure? Will some feel stigmatized? Will inequalities and differences, which concern many children, be made more overt and increase? Finally, can teachers both conduct such assessments and maintain the close rapport which has been such a distinctive characteristic of high-quality primary education in the past?

Whatever happens, teachers must, and will, try to sustain the quality of their relationships with their children, for reasons which will be discussed more fully in Chapter 4. Similarly, parents and governors must take particular care to ensure that the highlighting of children's needs and differences through more detailed, systematic assessment will not become the basis, even tacitly, of evaluative judgements about their worth. All children have equal rights to their dignity and to the fulfilment of their potential.

Ways of beginning to address such issues have been developed through the use of 'records of achievement' or having a 'portfolio' for each child. Records of achievement are based on the conviction that all children can do and achieve a great deal, albeit at a variety of levels and across diverse activities. Pupil records, it is argued, should thus positively emphasize the diversity and richness of what each child *can* do, rather than simply measure and record their levels of academic achievement by testing them to their point of failure. A record of achievement for a primary-aged child might take the form of a 'portfolio' in which material from the parents and child as well as the teacher can gradually be gathered. Through the evidence collected there, it can provide an accumulating record of successes and a profile of the child's characteristics in social and emotional terms as well as with regard to the more narrow academic concerns of reading, writing, mathematics, etc.

Such methods of recording and reporting children's achievements describe and celebrate the 'whole child' rather than just a narrow range of academic attributes, and there are likely to be many initiatives to establish such records of achievement in primary schools over the next few years.

Conclusion

The National Curriculum and assessment procedures introduced by the Education Reform Act 1988 produced the most radical changes in primary education this century. The curriculum framework increased breadth of provision and thus enriched the curricular experiences of many children, but it was unmanageable and had to be revised. Similarly, the assessment procedures were impractical and, even after revision, many teachers still consider aspects of them to be educationally flawed and unnecessary.

The welcome which has been offered to the revised National Curriculum, introduced from 1995, must therefore be tempered with caution. It is too early to say how it will affect children's learning. Moreover, we should not forget Alan Blyth's proposition that we have responsibilities as adults to provide an 'enabling' education for our children. If our curricular intervention between children's development and their experience causes problems, then we should be bold enough to change it.

Suggestions for further reading

For a lucid discussion of the thinking behind the National Curriculum and of the issues raised, read:

> Pring, R. (1995) *The New Curriculum*. London: Cassell (second edition).

For insights into previous images of 'good practice' in primary schools, see:

> Blenkin, G. V. and Kelly, A. V. (eds) (1993) *The Primary Curriculum in Action*. London: Harper and Row.

The most exciting book on assessment in recent years is:

> Drummond, M. J. (1993) *Assessing Children's Learning*. London: David Fulton.

The most comprehensive studies of the impact of the National Curriculum and assessment on primary school practices and pupil experiences are:

> Pollard, A., Broadfoot, P., Croll, P., Osborn, M. and Abbott, D. (1994) *Changing English Primary Schools? The Impact of the Education Reform Act at Key Stage One*. London: Cassell.

> Pollard, A. (ed.) (1994) *Look Before You Leap? Research Evidence on the Impact of the National Curriculum at Key Stage Two*. London: Tufnell Press.

Chapter 4

TEACHERS, TEACHING AND LEARNING

Very little of quality can happen in schools without skilled, knowledgeable and committed teachers. In this chapter we begin to consider these issues in some depth and also to review the implications for teaching of the three different models of learning which were introduced in Chapter 1.

The commitment, morale and supply of teachers

In the past decade or so teachers have sometimes felt rather misunderstood. As one headteacher recently put it 'teachers can work without money or recognition – but not both'. This neatly encapsulates two of the main issues involved in what, in the early 1990s, was a severe collapse in teacher morale.

Teacher morale declined in the early 1990s as the debates about educational reform developed, but many of the criticisms levelled at teachers in state schools were grossly unfair. Take, for instance, the question of educational standards in secondary education. As measured by the Government's own statistics on exam performance, standards have risen steadily over the past 20 years. The 1995 official report from Her Majesty's Chief Inspector of schools confirmed a continuing rise in attainment and quality of teaching. Thus GCSE passes at grades A to C rose from 46 per cent to 53 per cent from 1989 to 1994 and A levels at grades A to C rose from 43 per cent to 51 per cent. And yet the flow of criticism from government has sometimes seemed to have have been almost unrelenting. Indeed, the phrase 'discourse of derision' was coined (Ball, 1990) to describe it. Small wonder then that a Gallup poll in January 1994 showed that two-thirds of the public thought that educational standards were falling, despite the clear, official indication to the contrary.

A second example is provided by the common belief that teaching young children is a relatively easy job with the benefit of long holidays. In fact, research on teachers' working hours in 1991 has shown that teachers work extremely hard (Campbell and Neill, 1994). The average time worked was 53.6 hours per week in term time and 20 per cent spent over 60 hours per week on school work. Within this average working week, 45 per cent of the time was spent with pupils and the other 55 per cent was spent in preparation, marking, professional development, planning meetings, administration and other activities. Teachers worked almost six hours on average each weekend. Even if allowance for holidays is made, Campbell and Neill calculated that primary school teachers were working the equivalent of a 45-hour week through the year, a figure which is significantly greater than the 35-hour week norm for non-manual workers for the same period (Incomes Data Services, 1992).

Given such common misapprehensions about teaching, one might well wonder – why do people choose to teach? Of course, there are many people who drift into teaching and soon leave, but the vast majority of long-service primary school teachers are in teaching because of their commitment to children. The rewards of teaching have never been financial, instead they primarily lie in the pleasure and fulfilment which comes from developing a close rapport with young children and in seeing them develop both intellectually and socially.

Such rewards are intrinsic. They have long been intertwined as part of the art and science of the job and they reached their high point of expression as part of the 'child-centred' philosophy which developed after the Plowden Report of 1967. This intrinsic satisfaction of work with young children remains the basis of the commitment of many teachers (Osborn, 1996). It represents beliefs and values to which most have dedicated their professional lives. Indeed, in a sense, the closeness of relationships with children and belief in the value of such relationships for supporting children's learning tends to become part of many teachers' own personal identities.

Consider the feelings of these teachers, who were cited in a study by Jennifer Nias (1989):

> I enjoy a time when you've worked very hard with the child for maybe two or three weeks and they haven't understood a word of what you've been saying and suddenly the penny drops. You see that lovely smile and their whole face lights up and they say, 'Oh yes! I've got it now!' (p. 93).

> Having (a sense of being in a class together) isn't to do with curriculum, or ... anything, it's about feeling you're together. What goes on in a classroom is mostly about feelings, just as it is in life generally. Feelings are infinitely more important in guiding how people act than ideas are. You have to accept the importance of feelings, your own and theirs (the children's), or you will never be happy as a teacher (p. 184).

The difficulty faced by many teachers after the legislation of the late 1980s and early 1990s was that the nature of the job was thought to have changed. There were several main concerns. First, the tightening of curriculum control at the time reduced scope for teacher autonomy and use of judgement. Second, teachers feared that the assessment procedures could become divisive, impractical and intrude into their relationship with children. Third, changes in teacher management structures and processes altered the nature of the job as 'work', for instance through appraisal procedures and the imposition of detailed contracts to define the role. Fourth, there were worries about the cumulative effect of plans for the public reporting of assessment results, the local management of school budgets and a naive encouragement of parental choice of school. It was feared that these innovations might cause schools to ebb and flow in size, depending on over-simplified views of the services they provide. 'It's becoming more like a business than a school', was a common sentiment.

Most immediately though, the issue which concerned primary school teachers in the early 1990s was the pace of change. The National Curriculum and assessment procedures were radical, complex and had enormous implications for previous practice in schools. The speed with which they were introduced was such that it was almost impossible for most teachers to keep up.

As we saw in Chapter 3, the review of the National Curriculum and assessment arrangements, which took effect from September 1995, was an attempt to respond to such feelings and to work 'with the grain' of teacher professionalism. Thus the specification of subject content to be taught in the new National Curriculum is lighter, the use of teacher judgement is more significant in curriculum planning and remains vital in assessment, administrative requirements have been reduced and no further changes to the National Curriculum are to be introduced until at least the year 2000. It is to be hoped that teachers will again find more personal and professional fulfilment from their work in this new and more trusting period.

However, one consequence of the rapid changes and crisis in teacher morale in the early 1990s was that many teachers left the profession. If there is an economic upturn in the UK, problems in recruiting and training more teachers are likely. At the same time the number of pupils of primary school age is expected to rise through the 1990s, particularly in the inner cities and in newer towns. The result could be a shortage of suitable staff in some areas.

Teachers' professional education and training has traditionally been provided by universities and colleges working in partnership with schools. In England, from the mid-1980s, initial training was regulated by the Council for the Accreditation of Teacher Education (CATE) but in 1994, this was superseded by the Teacher Training Agency (TTA) which has a national planning role, accredits institutions to run courses, controls funding for teacher education and commissions research on teaching and teacher education. A number of new routes into teaching were also developed in the early 1990s. Some, such as the Licensed and Articled Teachers Schemes, were primarily designed for older graduates with skills or expertise to offer. Others were designed to ensure that initial training was thoroughly grounded in experience within schools. Thus School Centred Initial Teacher Training (SCITT) schemes were designed to be led by schools themselves with less participation by higher education institutions. For teachers who are already in post, staff development opportunities depend on what is offered in their school, what is available from local education providers and the annual focus of the government's national programme for training (GEST: Grants for Education Support and Training).

Despite the new attempts to being a calmer atmosphere to schools and the new initiatives to develop the quality of teachers, it does seem reasonable to suggest that a significant contribution to enhancing teacher commitment could simply be to respect and value the teachers we already have – as is done in most other parts of the world. A sustained lead from national policy-makers would almost certainly be very welcome. I wonder too what this would mean in terms of the staff of your school? You could enquire, for instance, into those 'hidden skills' of classroom organization and management.

Classroom organization and management

When you visit a busy primary school classroom, or hear about it from a child, it may be difficult to interpret what is going on. As a visitor, you may see what seems to be a bewildering array of people, activities, spaces, equipment, noise and colour. Similarly, as a parent listening to your child at home, you will probably need all the skills of Sherlock Holmes to construct an impression of classroom life from the disparate information and partial accounts which you are likely to get. Such complexity of activity could easily be misinterpreted, but creating an effective classroom in primary schools has many facets and necessitates establishing a framework for behaviour within which the teacher can teach and the children can be given an appropriate degree of autonomy. In 1987, Her Majesty's Inspectors of Schools described the 'characteristics of good classroom work' in the following way:

> In almost all cases first impressions were of an informality which typifies many primary classrooms. Closer investigation showed that the freedoms were not there by chance. They had been adopted for

a variety of interrelated reasons. For example, on those occasions when children were permitted to move about the classroom so that they had access to the materials they needed and ... so ... that they could use reference books, they were being taught, at the same time, to select from a range of materials, to behave responsibly, and to persevere with the task in hand while showing a proper consideration for others working in the same room. By these and other means a sense of self discipline was being nurtured (HMI, 1987, p. 32).

Such flexibly structured ways of working are not easy to achieve and the topic of classroom organization and management is one which has been fiercely debated following a government discussion paper known as 'Three Wise Men's Report' (Alexander, Rose and Woodhead, 1992). In particular, the view was expressed that primary school teachers need to tighten their classroom control to ensure more purposive *teaching* of pupils. A 1993 report from the Office for Standards in Education (OFSTED) conveyed the new emphasis. Thus 'better classroom practice' was deemed to be associated with the following organizational strategies:

Carefully planned and appropriate groupings of pupils,

A mixture of individual, group and whole-class teaching,

A manageable number of teaching groups and learning activities,

Carefully planned use of the teacher's time for giving instructions, teaching the whole class, individuals and groups, and moving between activities to instruct, question, explain and assess,

Planned use of the pupils' time including setting of realistic deadlines for the completion of work,

Clearly established classroom routines and systems (OFSTED, 1993, p. 23).

In this second account, the instructional and organizational role of the teacher is much more prominent, processes are to be more tightly framed and the role of the pupils is relatively taken for granted. However, it is important to remember that, above all, the purpose of classroom work is to ensure that children learn, and teachers' teaching must connect *with* them rather than simply be directed *at* them.

It is clear from these accounts that teachers do face a number of dilemmas and choices in making decisions on classroom organization and management. There is a wide variety of strategies and the key to effective teaching lies in knowing which strategy to adopt for which purpose.

It would be too complicated to attempt to describe all the possible forms of classroom organization here, but I will try to highlight the issues and principles which lie behind them. It should then be possible to use these in interpreting and forming a view about what is going on in the classrooms in your particular school.

The most important issue which teachers face is how, on an hour-by-hour basis, to provide worthwhile and meaningful learning tasks and activities for large numbers of children. There are both behavioural and instructional aspects of this.

Classroom behaviour

Certainly each child will be valued and cared for as an individual, but collectively children do pose a potential threat to maintaining an ordered learning environment.

In such circumstances it is obviously necessary to establish classroom rules, routines and discipline, and it is essential to maintain them. When an ordered classroom climate of this sort is created it enables teachers to begin to resolve the child management aspects of their role so that they can concentrate on teaching and learning processes. For instance, such things as sharpening pencils, approving visits to the toilet, tying shoe laces or providing paper can all be managed by good classroom organization and the establishment of expectations and routines. They can thus save a lot of a skilled teacher's time – time which is in very short supply given the normal class size of between 25 and 30 children.

The main principle which should underlie all such systems of rules and routines is to work with and through the children. If the children do not understand and accept the classroom organization and management system, they are likely to become discontented. They will then either withdraw individually, or, eventually, collectively disrupt it – and after all there are a lot of them! Thus, teachers, whilst taking responsibility for initiating and monitoring such structures, will routinely discuss and negotiate the rules, routines and expectations which they wish to establish and maintain. It is essential that the children are clear about the teacher's expectations so that shared understandings about 'how we do things here' can become established. Two particular characteristics of good classroom management and organization systems follow.

First, they should be *coherent*. There should be an internal consistency in the way the space, time, resources, people and activities are structured. Many parents who have organized children's birthday parties will know how difficult this is. You've built up to the high point with the candles but you can't find the matches. You really did think there was room in the lounge to play Blind Man's Buff. Wayne has decided he won't play with the girls. The children are just starting their ice-cream but parents are arriving to take them away. There are many such pitfalls in organizing groups of children. The important point though is not just that getting in a muddle is stressful for the adults; it is that it is confusing and disorientating for the children. This is exactly what must be avoided if they are to be positive about something as important as their learning.

The second vital characteristic of good management and organization systems in classrooms is that they should be accepted by the children as *legitimate*. The teacher needs to ensure that expectations are expressed clearly, so there are no misunderstandings; that the thinking and purpose behind the rules are discussed so that they are meaningful, and that expectations and rules are maintained in consistent and even-handed ways, so that both the structures and the teacher are regarded as being 'fair'.

If classroom organization and management systems are established and maintained in these ways, the structures can both liberate the teacher to teach and empower the children to learn. They can then all get on with the educational process, supported by shared understandings and routines. The result may take a number of forms, from the tightly framed order of a teacher-led, instructional lesson, to that hive of more self-directed pupil activity which often seems so bewildering to the external eye. These are just the overt, visible results of the rules and routines of the 'mini-societies' which are built up in each classroom.

Maintaining such complex classroom structures for behaviour, purposive order and discipline is an extremely skilful task. It depends on analysis and intuition, on knowing what has to be done and on having the sensitivity to empathize and negotiate with the children or the confidence to become more assertive when appropriate. On many occasions a creative leap of the imagination may be called for to rally the class and take the children forward. No wonder that primary school teachers have been likened to the concert conductors who have simultaneously to control and get the best from their great orchestras – a 'best' for teachers, of course, which must be seen in terms of the quality of the children's learning.

Classroom instruction

Understanding of the importance of appropriate classroom instruction has developed considerably in recent years. In particular, it has been argued that teachers are able to teach more effectively where they have high levels of subject knowledge and where they organize their classroom to provide an appropriate mixture of teaching methods. Among the judgements to be made by teachers are those concerning the repertoire of teaching approaches to be used, how to present a clear focus and targets for children's efforts, maintain the pace of teaching sessions, pitch tasks and learning challenges at appropriate levels and use all the available time effectively. Subject knowledge helps in assessing children's present levels of understanding, in selecting well-matched future tasks so that the curriculum is appropriately 'differentiated', and in providing instruction directly or through questioning.

To do this, teachers require very high levels of skill, knowledge and understanding which has to be deployed in classroom conditions. Neville Bennett has carried out influential work on this and has represented teaching skills as a cycle in which the teacher intentions are presented through tasks (see Figure 4.1).

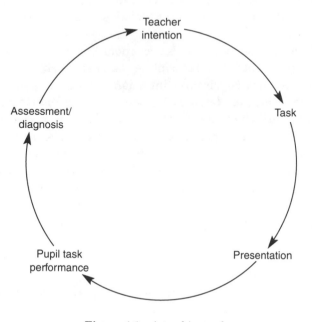

Figure 4.1   A teaching cycle

Source: Bennett (1987)

In recent years, primary school teachers have been gradually developing their subject knowledge of the new curriculum. However, there is a particular difficulty at Key Stage 2 where the full range of ten subjects of the National Curriculum plus religious education may be taught by one teacher, despite the increasingly detailed specification of each subject. At Key Stage 3 this teaching will be continued by a large team of secondary school specialist teachers, but the scale and funding disparities which affect primary education limit the extent to which moves in the direction of specialization have been attempted. Meanwhile, many primary school teachers necessarily have to work very hard to master the content of each of the National Curriculum subjects and to develop the full resources and skills to teach them.

For instance, although the Education Reform Act 1988 is very clear that teaching methods are to be decided by teachers exercising their professional judgement, teachers have been subject to a consistent line of criticism from Chris Woodhead, both before and after he was nominated in 1994, by the Conservative government of the time, to become Her Majesty's Chief Inspector of Schools. In a speech to the Royal Society of Arts, in January 1995, he argued that primary teachers hold 'woolly and simplistic' views of teaching and should increase their use of more traditional, 'chalk and talk' methods if they were not to compromise educational standards. However, there is no research evidence which establishes the superiority of this teaching approach. As Neville Bennett himself responded: 'Almost any method could be good or bad. There is no evidence that whole class teaching is any better or worse than any other kind. It can be brilliant and it can be bloody awful' (quoted in the *Independent*, 1 February 1995).

What research evidence is available emphasizes the importance of the exercise of professional judgement in deciding on the most appropriate teaching method for a particular learning goal. This is known as 'fitness for purpose' and it takes us back to the three psychological models which were first introduced in Chapter 1.

Adult roles in teaching and learning processes

As I suggested in the Introduction, learning goes on throughout our lives, particularly as we interact with and experience different people and things in our environment. The issues to be discussed below, about processes of teaching and learning, have thus been written with a wide range of forms of adult/ child interaction in mind. The issues do not just concern pupils and teachers for, as we have seen, parents are at least as significant in influencing the manner and content of children's learning.

In Chapter 1 the psychology of children's learning was introduced very simply and I suggested that *listening, doing* and *discussing* each play an important part in enabling a child to develop their knowledge, skills, concepts and attitudes. As I have suggested, an appropriate combination seems to be required and, because adults inevitably have a great deal of power and influence over interaction with children, it is essential that the adult role is very carefully considered. The three main psychological approaches to learning which have been discussed each have different implications for how adults should conduct themselves. I will illustrate these by adapting some models which were first devised by Stephen Rowland in an article called 'Child in Control' (Rowland, 1987).

The behaviourist model, emphasizing listening and based on a stimulus and response chain, might be represented by Figure 4.2.

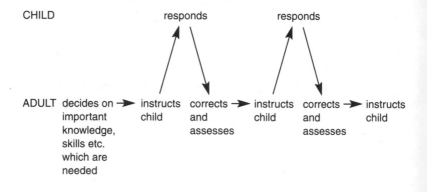

Figure 4.2 A behaviourist model of a teaching and learning process

On the other hand, Figure 4.3 represents the constructivist model, based on child-centred interpretations of Piaget's work.

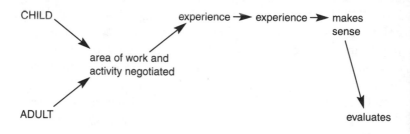

Figure 4.3 A constructivist model of a teaching and learning process

These two models present the adult role in quite different ways. In the former, control of the learning process is firmly in the hands of the adult and the child must respond as he or she best can. He or she is placed, essentially, in a passive role. In the second model, once the activity has been negotiated, each child is off on their own, on the argument that they need direct, personal experience and only they can construct their own understanding. The adult role here is to provide a rich and stimulating environment for the children to investigate and to which they will respond. Children may thus be very active and creative, but some could also lose their sense of purpose or even become bewildered. While the behaviourist model may fail to capitalize on the abilities and competence of children, the simple constructivist model risks failing to draw fully on the knowledge and expertise of adults.

I expect we can all think of times when our own behaviour illustrates such models. For instance, in my own family, when trying to get my two children ready to go to primary school in the morning I was often extremely directive. I appeared to think that my son and daughter would learn to get their shoes and coats on if I instructed them to do so and if I told them off when they didn't. Some chance! On the other hand, when my wife and I got home after work and we were tired, the children often asked if they could do something – make a go-cart, have a water-bomb fight, watch *Neighbours* – and, having negotiated terms, we tended to leave them to it – to explore in the garage, soak each other in the garden or goggle at the box. It wasn't very consistent was it? Sometimes directive; at other times permissive. But was it a contextually appropriate use of strategies? Perhaps we should not worry too much about using a full range of strategies, for children are very clever when they need to be and they become extremely good at diagnosing the mood of adults and the 'rules in play' in different learning situations.

I would argue that the optimal learning model must build on all that adults and children have to offer. There must be activity on both sides but, because it is essentially true that children can only build genuine understanding in their own minds, they must have a considerable degree of opportunity and control. The role of the adult then becomes to support, excite, instruct, scaffold and extend their thinking. Thus we have a model, such as the one in Figure 4.4 and which I will call 'social constructivist'.

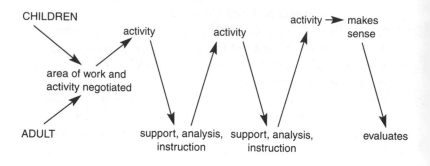

Figure 4.4   A social constructivist model of a teaching and learning process

Here children and adult share ideas and talk together to agree a goal. The adult may provide some instruction or initial guidance at that point. The children then begin the activity whilst the adult draws back a little. The children thus have the space they need to exert control within the activity, to try things out and to define difficulties for themselves. However, the adult is available and can reflect on what is happening so that the child can be supported if necessary. If the children identify a need, the adult is ready. He or she can offer questions, information or resources, suggest new strategies or provide other forms of instruction. This is where the children are 'scaffolded' across their appropriate 'zone of proximal development', that extension of their understanding or skill which they can reach if appropriately supported. The children continue the activity at a new level and finally the adult and children join together to discuss and review what has been achieved.

Many conditions have to be right to make this model work. As you will know from your own family, such sequences may almost naturally occur when people are feeling reasonably relaxed and sure of each other, if the children act responsibly and if the adult gives them both space and support as appropriate. However, they may also be created more proactively in situations when a teacher provides instruction to a whole class and structured follow-up tasks and is then able to respond to pupil needs as they arise and to challenge, support and extend the children's understanding.

Primary school teachers are increasingly working on variants of this social constructivist model – though they may not always analyse it as I have presented it here. Why not try enquiring about your school's approach to science, maths, writing or design technology?

Some of the best forms of modern practice are based on children working in groups on collectively agreed problems and tasks with the teacher monitoring their activity and discussing and supporting them as appropriate. Perhaps they share a single task together or the activity may be set up so that they each contribute a distinct element towards a collective goal. Such collaborative learning develops communicative and social skills in addition to the extension of knowledge and understanding, as the National Oracy Project (1990) showed. Figure 4.5 illustrates the overlapping nature of these processes.

The case study below, of a teacher's development of some topic work with her class, illustrates a type of pedagogy which is associated with the social contructivist model and used a 'jigsaw' form of collaborative learning to produce a large, three-dimensional classroom display.

Designing a playground for toys – an illustration of teaching and learning processes

This case study is based on the work of a class of 5- and 6-year-olds from an inner-city school who were doing a topic on 'toys'. As you read it, you could try to relate it to the social constructivist model described above.

One summer morning, the children, their teacher and some parents travelled by bus to visit a local stately home where they were to study a collection of Victorian toys. Historical, geographical and linguistic aspects of the topic had

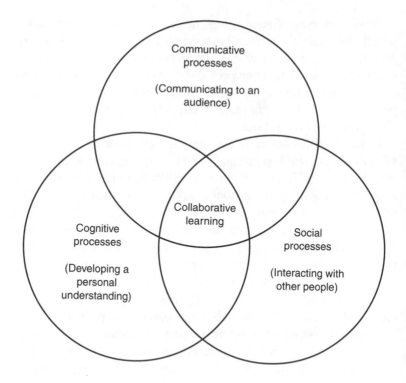

Figure 4.5 A representation of the process involved in collaborative learning

already been given some emphasis and the teacher therefore particularly wanted to develop the children's interests in ways which could lead them into technological, scientific and mathematical activity.

Whilst touring the exhibits, questions about the materials and construction of the toys were raised by the adults. Discussion about how these compared with modern toys developed and detailed observational drawings were made.

At lunch time the children had a picnic in the grounds and were given an opportunity to use the playground. There were swings, a roundabout, tumble-barrels, slides and climbing frames of various sorts. As they played, some children commented, 'Hey, these are very big toys!' and discussions ensued about the materials and construction of the playground apparatus.

This is the point where the flexibility and creativity of a good primary school teacher comes in. The teacher realized that the children were beginning to transfer their understanding of new and old small toys to a new situation. There was a possibility of extending the project and achieving broader curricular aims on grounds of the children's own choosing. After their play the teacher gathered the children together in a circle for a discussion. She explained that, since they were interested in the playground equipment, she would like the children to take paper and pencil and make a very detailed drawing of one piece of apparatus, paying particular attention to what it was made of and how the bits were joined together. An example of one child's work is provided in Figure 4.6.

Figure 4.6 A child's drawing of playground equipment

On the way back to school in the bus there was further discussion between teacher and children, and it was decided that it would be good to 'make a playground for the play people' (plastic toys) and that it could be set out on a big sheet of paper.

On the next day the work began. The children were asked to think about how playground apparatus was made and to make a design for their model. To help them in this, various materials were made available – light wooden rods of 1 cm square section, paper, glue, cotton reels, small pieces of wood, string, nails, screws, etc. With a good deal of discussion, the children drew up their plans of swings, roundabouts, tumble-barrels and climbing frames. One of these, for a tumble-barrel and drawn in profile, is reproduced in Figure 4.7.

Figure 4.7 A child's plan for a tumble-barrel

One may well have difficulty in interpreting this design! Remember these children were only 5 years old and they were right at the beginning of their school learning, for instance, learning how to write. However, this little boy was making very sound progress. The 'S' on each side of the design indicates screws which were to provide axles for two cotton reels and thus produce a double tumble-barrel. This was to be held up on rods which were to be mounted on a base. This base was to be made from '2BUW' – that is, 'two bits of wood!'

This is an illustration of 'emergent writing' – a process of development endorsed by the National Curriculum, in which children are encouraged to write to communicate in meaningful situations. Writing is to be 'real', purposeful and the children's own. As we have seen, spelling is likely to be somewhat idiosyncratic in the early stages but, by producing drafts of writing and sharing and discussing them with others, this develops until adult conventions are observed.

The plans which were drawn engendered much discussion among the children, about scale, the materials to be used and about whether they would 'work'. Some plans were revised in the light of this group learning.

Simple tools were then introduced, saws, screwdrivers, hammers, nails, scissors, glue-sticks – and the children began to implement their plans. As they worked the teacher circulated, watching, and encouraging. From time to time a problem would arise – 'my rods won't stay up', 'some of these bits are too short', 'how can we fix this?' 'Will this swing OK?' 'Can a play person fit on here?' Many of such problems and questions were resolved by the children themselves but the teacher was on hand to meet their needs when called for. She was able to show them a necessary technique for reinforcing butt-jointed wooden rods (with triangular card glued at each side), she was able to point to equipment which would help – 'How about using a ruler to measure with?' Above all, she was able to ask appropriate questions.

Asking questions of children is, as an adult, a very difficult thing to do well. We tend either to feed children with the right answer or to set up instant 'tests' in which children often feel vulnerable. Either of these ways is essentially disabling to the child. From the first method they learn to borrow other peoples' answers and from the second they learn that it pays not to ask at all. The knack for adults is thus to ask questions which lead children on, which point them in appropriate directions, but which have enough openness to allow them to think for themselves. Appropriate questions, followed by giving children time to try things out again, are a main contribution to scaffolding children's understanding.

The construction process continued, on and off for over a week, as problems were faced, discussed and overcome and as the children's plans began to be realized as models. All the time there was a constant process of interaction between the children and the teacher as she facilitated the learning which the children controlled. As the number of completed models grew, a need to produce a layout for the playground was agreed and this was produced on a roll of wide paper. After animated discussions, about such things as how much space there should be around the swings and where the paths would go best, a group of children undertook to draw the layout. When a final version was agreed, other children coloured it in and the playground models could finally be set in place.

Over the remaining weeks of the term the children played with this toy playground which they had collectively created. It stimulated further reading and writing, and more design and technological realization. It raised childrens' awareness about materials and their confidence in what they, themselves, could achieve.

This example illustrates the way in which good primary practice works through, with and alongside children. The teacher provides essential structure and guidance, not to mention the ultimate disciplinary boundaries, but the children can make learning their own only when they are given real opportunities.

Such work is also clearly within the terms of the National Curriculum. From reference to Table 3.3 on page 46, in which the attainment targets for each subject are set out, you will see how this work on making a playground for toys directly relates to it. Regarding English, there was a great deal of purposive speaking and listening and early attempts at writing were stimulated. In terms of art, investigating and making were practised as the children attempted to represent the playground through their plans and models. Maths was applied through the measurement of materials used for the models and scientific activity embraced three areas of the programme of study: experimental and investigative science, materials and their properties and physical processes. Perhaps the strongest focus though was on technology, in which designing and making provide the two key elements of the curriculum. Such an analysis, in more detail, went into the teacher record so that the breadth and progression of children's work could be monitored over a much longer period as the children engage in a succession of activities. Work on these attainment targets is summarized in Table 4.1.

Table 4.1   National Curriculum attainment targets addressed by the children's work on designing a playground for toys

English	Maths	Science	Technology	Art
AT1	AT1	AT1	AT1	AT1
AT3	AT2	AT3	AT2	
	AT3	AT4		

Conclusion

As this chapter has progressed, we have seen how the commitment, knowledge and skills of teachers provide vital support to children as they progressively explore the world and seek to understand it.

Teachers have the opportunity and power to facilitate children's learning very positively. They can also sometimes inhibit it. The latter is particularly likely if class management and organization are weak or if the very wide-ranging demands placed on teachers result in an overcrowded or poorly matched programme of activities which fails to challenge children adequately. Teachers must combine subject knowledge with sensitivity to pupils' social and emotional needs as learners. In most instances however, the creativity, skill and understanding of primary school teachers, given the resources available to them, is a considerable professional achievement.

Suggestions for further reading

Some very interesting and perceptive insights regarding teaching and teachers are provided by:

Nias, J. (1989) *Primary Teachers Talking*. London: Routledge.

Cortazzi, M. (1990) *Primary Teaching: How it Is*. London: David Fulton.

For a detailed study of teachers' work, see:

Campbell, R. J. and Neill, S. R. St. J. (1994) *Primary Teachers at Work*. London: Routledge.

For a more general overview of the main issues to do with teachers and teaching, see:

Delamont, S. (1987) *The Primary School Teacher*. London: Falmer.

Books which analyse all the major skills involved in teaching and suggest ways of developing them are:

Pollard, A. and Tann, S. (1993) *Reflective Teaching in the Primary School*. London: Cassell (second edition).

Clegg, D. and Billington, S. (1994) *The Effective Primary Classroom*. London: David Fulton.

The following book engages with the big debate in primary education about 'child-centredness' and argues for more teacher-centred approaches:

McNamara, D. (1994) *Classroom Pedagogy and Primary Practice*. London: Routledge.

But teacher creativity and responsiveness to children remain important, as Peter Woods demonstrates:

Woods, P. (1995) *Creative Teachers in Primary Schools*. Milton Keynes: Open University Press.

Chapter 5
PARENTS AND CHILDREN'S LEARNING

This chapter concerns the benefits – and challenges – of parents and teachers working together in the interests of children's learning. It begins with a discussion of some of the key issues which face any adult seeking to help children learn and suggests the particularly important role of parents in building self-confidence. This is followed by an analysis of some of the potential tensions in home-school relationships and of the contradictions between parents' roles when they are seen as 'consumers' and as 'partners'. Types and degrees of involvement in school life are then considered and the chapter concludes with views of some children themselves about *their* involvement in parent-teacher liaison.

Supporting children learning

A helpful insight into aspects of the parental role in supporting children's learning has been provided by Peter Hannon. He suggests that parents can provide:

Opportunities for learning such as investigative, expressive and play equipment, fiction and non-fiction books and, in particular, a wide range of experiences,

Recognition of each part of their child's achievements through praise and reinforcement,

Interaction in which parents spend time with their child, talking, explaining and challenging them to new learning,

Modelling through which parents demonstrate the uses, enjoyment and benefits which can arise from skills which have been learned (Hannon, 1995, p. 51).

Thus, if we take early literacy for instance, children need numerous opportunities to express themselves, to develop their spoken language, to enjoy stories, poems, to appreciate the uses of print around them and to explore ways of representing ideas on paper, however simply. Their efforts in all this need recognition and praise and also the guidance which will come from interaction with their parents. If uses of literacy are apparent from the ways in which parents speak, read and write within the home, such modelling will also enable the child to understand the multiple purposes of his or her learning and to generate high expectations. Of these four forms of support, parents' role in interaction with their children is particularly subtle and it is on this that we focus below.

We saw in Chapter 4 how all adults can play a crucial part in supporting children's learning during activities. Teachers aim to 'scaffold children's understanding' with sensitive and appropriately judged challenges, questions and resources. So it is for parents too. Consider, for instance, this short transcript of everyday conversation between a mother and her 4-year-old daughter:

Child: Is our roof a sloping roof?

Mother: Mmm. We've got two sloping roofs, and they sort of meet in the middle.

Child: Why have we?

Mother: Oh, its just the way our house is built. Most people have sloping roofs, so that the rain can run off them. Otherwise, if you have a flat roof, the rain would sit in the middle of the roof and make a big puddle, and then it would start coming through.

Child: Our school has a flat roof, you know.

Mother: Yes it does actually, doesn't it?

Child: And the rain sits there and goes through?

Mother: Well, it doesn't go through. It's probably built with drains so that the water runs away. You have big blocks of flats with rather flat sort of roofs. But houses that were built at the same time this house was built usually had sloping roofs.

Child: Does Lara have a sloping roof? (Lara is a friend.)

Mother: Mmm. Lara's house is very like ours. In countries where they have a lot of snow they have even more sloping roofs. So that when they've got a lot of snow, the snow can just fall off.

Child: Whereas, if you have a flat roof, what would it do? Would it just have a drain?

Mother: No, then it would sit on the roof, and when it melted it would make a big puddle.

In this extract from an excellent book by Barbara Tizard and Martin Hughes (1984), we can clearly see the active process of 'intellectual search' which characterizes part of the competence of young children. This process of thinking and questioning is an important contribution to learning and benefits from the support of an adult. For instance, the mother receives questions openly, participates in the exchange and offers advice in ways which facilitate the child's attempt to understand. The child's process of enquiry is directly supported, though interestingly we can also see here how easy it is to begin to mislead children when we underestimate the clarity and accuracy of the responses which are needed. We can note too, how the mother's contribution relates quite closely to the social constructivist model reviewed on page 75.

Appropriate parental support for children in particular learning situations is clearly very important and opportunities to develop the quality and effectiveness of what we try to do for our children occur all the time – learning to swim, to catch, to play music, to conduct oneself appropriately in public, etc. The possibilities occur daily and in many routine situations. Indeed, simple, unpressured times are often particularly productive for the conversations which support learning. They may occur at bathtimes, while going for a walk, or doing routine household chores, in fact in any situation in which 'space' exists in which the *child* can initiate, ask questions and control his or her process of 'intellectual search'. Some examples might be relatively straightforward:

- Does 5 add 5 make ten?
- Why is the sky blue?
- What keeps my heart beating?
- Is Santa Claus real?

Other questions can be more difficult:

- Will 'Goldie' go to Heaven?
- How do I know if I'm in a dream or not?

- Why doesn't Marie like me?
- Why don't people in Africa have more to eat?

How are such questions to be answered? They express a need, a desire for more information and guidance, so that the next element in the construction of understanding can be acquired.

The most difficult issue for parents concerns how we support our children when they reach the present limits of their skill or understanding. When they approach their zone of proximal development' (see pages 11–13 and Figure 1.1), how do we ensure that they avoid a sense of confusion or failure, with the risk of withdrawal or demoralization? How do we guide them without interfering too much? How do we provide instruction yet ensure that genuine space remains in which they can develop their own understanding?

Here is an example of a mother explaining how her husband had encouraged her 6-year-old to have more confidence in herself in the early stages of her reading:

> Something happened the other day, something to do with reading. Rob was bathing them and putting them to bed one night. Hazel said, 'Dad, you're really good at teaching me'. Because he'd said that, 'when you can't find a word sometimes there's clues in the picture', and she'd got stuck on a word and he'd said, 'well, what's the picture about?' and she'd said the word. She must have been aware of it before but perhaps not put like that. And Rob had said to her, 'Well, you're good at teaching yourself. You're the best person, you're the one that's learning and picking these things up'. And just then she picked up one of her other books, 'Scarry's treasure' or something, that *we'd* always read to her in the past, and she picked it up and realised that she could read books that we had previously read to her. And she'd never really twigged that before, except for some very simple ones.
>
> She thought it was fantastic. Took a book to bed with her and every time she got stuck on a word she'd shout, 'Mum, what's this word?' until eventually I had to take it off her because it was getting so late.
>
> Hazel is actually reading other books now, even though she doesn't understand the larger words. And she was so proud of herself that she could actually pick up this other book, I mean, I know she's not the best reader in the world, but she's not bad now and I think if she

comes on the way she has been doing, it will be fantastic (Hazel's mother, quoted in Pollard with Filer, 1995).

Hazel's parents clearly caught the right moment for their daughter. The father encouraged her to think about what she could do in a new way and her mother followed up with more support, instruction and praise so that a 'breakthrough' occurred. Hazel's sense of dependence and of uncertainty was replaced with a new confidence in herself and in her ability to read.

Children learning at the limits of their understanding and skill thus pose a particular challenge, for they are vulnerable both intellectually and emotionally. There is a real risk of misunderstanding and of demotivation. Like Hazel's parents, our task is to recognize these crucial moments and to support the children's learning. This ability to scaffold children across their zone of proximal development – to support their next learning increment – is the hallmark of a good teacher, be they at home or at school.

Parents however, also have another very significant role to play. Young children reflect their biographies, – their family, home, language and culture – as they approach their work in school. They reflect their emergent 'selves' as unique individuals, with particular characteristics and patterns of previous experience. They have been exposed to a particular range of experiences – of different creative media, of social and cultural situations, of language and literature, of different environments and activities. How then, have they learned to relate with others and begun to view themselves? This question is of vital importance for learning and for much else besides, because it concerns coming to terms with oneself within one's society. The 'I', of semi-unconscious feeling about oneself, gradually comes to terms with the 'me' – the more conscious sense of 'self' which is defined by the reactions of others and by personal reflection. Look again at the example from Hazel above, in which, as much as anything, she was encouraged to believe in herself as an active learner. Could you really separate this social and emotional development from her cognitive achievement?

Play is particularly important in this for young children because it provides opportunities for them to try out a variety of roles – to experiment with self-presentation and to gradually begin to stabilize their presentation of self into the core nature of the person they will become. Over time, this stabilization process reaches a point where it becomes appropriate to speak of a 'substantial self' having formed. The person then has a relatively constant view of themselves, and characteristic ways of thinking, relating and acting. Clearly this process develops throughout children's lives at home and at school. It is likely though, that home life is of much greater significance than any other with parents *mediating* and helping their child to interpret and make sense of their diverse other experiences as they accumulate (Pollard with Filer, 1995).

One outcome of this process, which is of particular importance to us here, is that each child is likely to develop a particular set of attitudes and perspectives on learning. A useful way of summarizing this is provided by the notion of 'learning stance', a concept which describes any relatively consistent patterns in the ways in which young children approach their learning. For some, every day is a new opportunity to be seized. For others school life is something which simply happens to them, something which they have to bear. To illustrate this, we can think back to Chapter 1 and to the ways in which Sally and Daniel approached school life at the age of 6. Sally seemed far more sure of herself, in her family, at school and with her peers. She approached her work eagerly and with a determination to succeed. Daniel was more tentative. He was more unsure of his place in his family, nervous of the teachers with whom he was placed and on the periphery of the friendship groups of his child contemporaries at school. His learning stance was often wary and uncertain.

Two practical policy aims for parents follow from this discussion. First, *that everything possible should be done to help children develop a positive sense of their own ability to learn.* A constructive learning stance is based on self-confidence, a spirit of enquiry, an openness to accept risk of failure and a determination to overcome difficulties that arise. A 3-year-old happily singing a new nursery rhyme to Granny, can thus be seen as building the foundation for a self-confident approach to new challenges in later life.

Second, *that the educational expectations between home and school should be respectful and as consistent as possible.* As children gradually develop their sense of self from interaction with others they are greatly advantaged by continuity and stability. As we shall see, there are also particular benefits for learning when parents and teachers work closely together on specific aspects of the curriculum (such as reading).

We have thus established the vital role of parents in helping their children with specific learning activities, influencing self-confidence and the learning stance which each child adopts and in providing expectations to which they may aspire. We now move to consider the relationship between home and school in more detail for, regrettably, it is a much more difficult relationship in practice than the theory of how children learn suggests it should be.

Relationships between home and school

In principle, the argument for a close working 'partnership' between parents and teachers is unassailable. Where it occurs it is clearly beneficial to the children's learning and experience. However, it is often difficult to achieve because of two fundamental tensions that affect the relationship. The first concerns the different primary responsibilities of parents and teachers and the second concerns the exercise of power and control over school practices.

Primary responsibilities

Put starkly it is a basic truth that parents tend to be primarily concerned for their own individual children. Our interest as parents is thus relatively specific. A teacher must, professionally, have a wider range of concerns. Their interests must embrace all the children and their collective entitlement to education.

Teaching, of course, is a far from easy job – a job in which expectations and needs far outstrip the time and resources made available to meet them. It thus poses many dilemmas, some of which are listed in Table 5.1.

Table 5.1 Common dilemmas faced by teachers (from Pollard and Tann, 1993, Reflective Teaching in the Primary School)

Treating each child as a 'whole person	Treating each child primarily as a 'pupil'
Organising the children on an individual basis	Organising the children as a class
Giving children a degree of control over their use of time, their activities and their work standards	Tightening control over children's use of time, their activities and their work standards
Seeking to motivate the children through intrinsic involvement and enjoyment of activities	Offering reasons and rewards so that children are extrinsically motivated to tackle tasks
Developing and negotiating the curriculum based on an appreciation of children's interests	Providing a subject curriculum which a national curriculum specifies and which 'society' expects them to receive
Attempting to integrate various subjects of the curriculum	Dealing systematically with each discrete subject of the curriculum
Aiming for quality in school work	Aiming for quantity in school work
Focusing on basic skills or on cognitive development	Focusing on expressive or creative areas of the curriculum
Trying to build up co-operative and social skills	Developing self-reliance and self-confidence in individuals
Inducting the children into a common culture	Affirming the variety of cultures in a multi-ethnic society
Allocating teacher time, attention and resources equally among all the children	Paying attention to the special needs of particular children
Maintaining consistent rules and understandings about behaviour and school work	Being flexible and responsive to particular situations
Presenting oneself formally to the children	Relaxing with the children
Working with professional application- and care for the children	Working with consideration of one's personal needs

If one thinks of the needs of a particular individual child, deciding the best way to resolve such dilemmas may seem relatively straightforward. The appropriate course of action often appears to be blindingly obvious – and so it often seems to parents who have identified a particular need for their child. 'If only the teacher would do ... ', we might say – and we may be right. The problem comes when we also think about the needs of the other children, about the political pressure and legal constraints which are imposed on teachers and about the limited resources which are available to them. Resolving such dilemmas and forming a judgement about the best course of action then becomes much more difficult. It becomes, in the opinion of most teachers, a professional matter. The judgement then has to be made by teachers who draw on their training, their wide-ranging comparative experience and on consultation with other people with legitimate interests or appropriate expertise.

Clearly one can, as a parent, understand all these issues and accept these proper professional concerns but still be dissatisfied at the outcome. Indeed, it is highly unlikely that the school to which we send our children will provide precisely what we judge is appropriate for our children at every point. We, as parents, can thus only really relax if we can move to a position in which we begin to trust the school and in which we put our specific concerns into a wider perspective.

This brings us to the second issue which makes an element of tension between home and school almost inevitable – the issue of power and control.

Power and control of schools

There have been very rapid changes concerning the control of schools in recent years. The Education Act 1944 was implemented towards the end of the war at a time when there was an unusual degree of consensus and solidarity in our society. It was distinctive for the way in which it assumed an implicit partnership between people at all levels of the education service, including teachers and parents. It was a time too though, in which considerable autonomy for teachers was expected, roles were delineated and due deference to teachers' professional judgement was accepted. The economic crises of the 1970s challenged these assumptions and led to questions being asked about the relationship between the education system and economic and social needs. Following this, the legislation of 1980, 1981, 1986, 1988 and 1993 radically changed the nature of parent-teacher relationships. Parents now have considerably more legal rights and there are a number of ways for parents to exercise influence over school practices.

Among the rights that parents now enjoy are those designed to provide for more choice between schools, for detailed reports on children's attainment through the National Curriculum and for greater representation on the governing body of the schools which their children attend. The latter is the most direct way of exercising power for it is to the school's governors that teachers are now primarily accountable and it is the school's governors who set the policy frameworks within which teachers must act. Power can also be exercised indirectly however. For instance, there is no doubt that the informal views of parents about different schools which are formed in day-to-day social discussions – over coffee, at the school gate waiting to collect the children, at the pub, etc – have an influence on school practices because of their potential effect on enrolment numbers.

The Education Reform Act 1988 provided the legislative underpinning of this move from parents as largely passive 'users' of education to be cast in a new role as potentially active 'consumers'. The emphasis was placed squarely on parents as clients of schools who make choices and thus exercise power in much the same way as consumers do in a market for goods. The 'Parent's Charter' was first issued in 1991 and this set out parental rights to choose a school for their child and to be provided with a range of information about schools and about their child's progress. However, the provision of parental choice remains somewhat rhetorical since popular schools are often unable to offer places. The number of parents using the appeals procedure to try to secure entry for their child to their chosen school has risen enormously since 1989 and there does seem to be a trend towards popular schools, in effect, selecting pupils rather than simply being able to respond to parental wishes. Teachers and classrooms cannot be provided and removed fast enough to produce an entirely responsive supply of education in schools where parents want or do not want them. Nor did the Parent's Charter offer any guarantees on resources or quality. As parents in the Campaign for State Education put it: 'The Parent's Charter is "a monstrous confidence trick and a wicked waste of public money" (despite the fact that it was distributed to 20 million homes) providing "no assurance to parents of their right to adequate staffing, properly qualified teachers and equipment to implement the National Curriculum"' (cited in *Education*, 17 June 1994).

It is also worth noting that parental satisfaction with the primary schools which their children attend tends to be very high. A 1989 government survey found that 94 per cent of parents were 'very' or 'fairly satisfied', and a similar proportion of contented parents was found in a more recent independent study (Hughes *et al.* 1994).

Nevertheless, the Conservative governments of the early 1990s believed that new parental rights and legal structures would produce higher educational standards through a beneficial process of competition among schools in a locality. More time is needed to trace the consequences of this policy, but the fear which some people have continued to hold in the mid-1990s is that systems for the provision of services to people are not so simply amenable to management by market forces. On the one hand, there are long-term investment and strategic planning issues which have previously been the responsibility of Local Education Authorities. On the other hand there are questions about the experience of children in the midst of the cut and thrust of competition. In particular, what of children in less popular schools whose parents, perhaps without transport, are unable to exercise choice? If more mobile children are moved, then funding for the school will be reduced and the school may find it more difficult to implement its development plans. Rather than ratcheting standards up, this produces a danger of initiating a cycle of decline for some schools.

The basic question is: Is the application of a 'market model' appropriate for education? Competing stallholders in a fruit and vegetable market are likely to find that the produce which people judge to be 'best' will sell quickly. This may well spur other traders to improve their quality and, to that extent, the Government's case is supported. However, stallholders where sales of fruit are low are likely to have less to invest and may find themselves forced out of business. In a fruit and vegetable market this may not matter much (unless you happen to be the stallholder under pressure) because consumers can easily find alternatives. However, schools serve particular, specific communities and, for many people, real opportunities for travel and for choice between schools are very limited. Thus, whilst parental rights may enable greater choice for some, they could also reduce the quality of what is available for others. Some people do have to buy substandard fruit and vegetables when their local shop is the only one to which they can travel. In the future then, some children may have to suffer the consequences of other people's choices in ways which will seriously disadvantage them.

However, there is also the question of whether parents will actually accept the consumerist role into which they have been cast. There are some signs that they may not, particularly when the difficult circumstances faced by state maintained schools become apparent. A good example of this is the concern about class size in primary schools. Class sizes rose from a relative low point in 1984 to reach an average of 26.9 children per primary classroom by 1994. However, by then no less than 28 per cent of all primary school pupils, 1.1 million, were in classes of 30 or over. The parents of these children were not at all pleased and they began to pressurize government for more resources. Ministers suggested that the effects of class size were unproven but, as a parent in an opinion survey put it: 'Any halfwit should realise that increasing class size is detrimental to a child's education' (cited in Bennett, 1994, p. 24).

In early 1995, the government proposed a grant to Local Education Authorities for 1995–96 which was insufficient to fund the educational salaries bill, and which was expected to lead to teacher redundancies and a further increase in class sizes. As a result, there were mass protests and parents and others on many governing bodies resigned to signal their dismay. Teachers, governors and parents may thus unite over such issues and, in such ways, ally to move beyond the market model which seems to be designed to divide them.

In summary then, there is little doubt of the value of a close partnership in the education of young children between parents and teachers, the community and schools. On the other hand the consumerist assumptions which underpinned legislation in the early 1990s will structure our actions as we approach the millennium and could undercut the development of such close forms of involvement. Teachers who are being held formally and publicly accountable may become more insular rather than open themselves up. Schools which are placed in competition with each other may wish to develop internally rather than share ideas and co-operate with other colleagues. We do not yet know what the outcome will be, or how this contradiction between partnership and consumerism will be resolved. In a sense, it is up to all those who use or work in education.

With this in mind we now go on to consider some of the different types of involvement in school life and children's learning which are open to parents.

Involvement in school life and children's learning

The easiest way to think about this is in terms of the degree of potential involvement in the learning process. For purposes of discussion, we can thus identify four types of involvement, as in Figure 5.1.

Low involvement ◄····························► High involvement
in the learning process   in the learning process

| Parents as clients | Parents as resources | Parents as participants | Parents as partners |

Figure 5.1 Four forms of parental involvement in schools

Parents as clients

This is a non-participation model and it may be adopted for a number of reasons. Perhaps the school wishes to discourage parental involvement – for this was the norm even in primary schools at one time. Non-participation is also the model of parental participation which best fits a consumerist philosophy in which education is treated as a commodity to be traded. In this perspective schools provide a service and are subject to inspection and assessment procedures so that quality and achievement can be gauged. With these assurances, parents then leave schools to get on with educating their children, but they do have appropriate consumer rights such as receiving reports, making complaints, etc. Other parents may adopt a non-participation role for quite different reasons. Perhaps they are in full-time employment, have a limited command of English or are hesitant about approaching schools because of something in their own previous educational experience.

From a school's point of view, parental non-participation is thus hard to interpret. It is certainly not clear if teachers' work is being valued if little feedback is given by parents, and in such circumstances teachers must draw on their professional convictions as they seek to do their best for the children.

On the other hand, there are schools which treat parents as non-participatory clients, whether the parents want it or not. Such schools can make it very difficult for parents to become involved in the learning of their children. One example of this (and one which is a good indicator of the policy of a school on this issue generally) is the way in which feedback is given to parents about their children's progress. At some schools it is routine practice to allow a five- or ten-minute period for each child's parents at a 'Parents' Evening' once or twice each year. Teachers use this time to deliver a verbal report about each child's progress whilst monitoring their watches to maintain their schedule. Whatever the reasons for such provision (and we must accept that there are many), it offers only a modest opportunity for genuine dialogue by which parents can join with teachers in a sustained educational partnership in the interests of the children.

The reports to parents which schools provide are welcome records of progress but they are rarely formative and they thus offer only limited opportunities for parents to become involved directly in supporting their children's development.

Parents as resources

Because of the financial pressures on schools, headteachers have always been keen to gather resources from willing parents in a variety of ways. We can distinguish between three types of parental resource – as fund-raisers, as experts and as helpers doing jobs in school.

As *fund-raisers* parents have been making an increasingly significant contribution to school budgets. HMI showed in 1986 that many primary schools received more money from parental contributions towards 'capitation' costs (expenditure for educational equipment and everyday consumables) than was provided by local authorities and this has continued to develop. In 1994 the National Association of Headteachers estimated that parental contributions in England and Wales totalled almost £200 million and reported that one exceptional primary school was benefiting by £16,000 per annum. Parent Teacher Associations and other forms of parent organization can thus, through fêtes, jumble sales, sponsored walks, covenants, etc, act as an enormous material asset for the school by simply raising money. Whilst such support is obviously very welcome, an important point of principle is also involved here. Since our education system is based on an expectation of entitlement for all children, it can be seen as unjust if some schools in well-off areas are able to resource themselves significantly better than schools serving less affluent communities. Given the existing range of such income from a few hundred to many thousands of pounds, this is an issue which should be faced by government.

As *experts*, parents, and other members of the community, are often drawn into the work of schools. Contributions to the development of curriculum topics are particularly common. Nurses, farm workers, postal staff, bricklayers, miners, community artists, writers and even an engine and crew from the fire brigade are all examples of parental experience being drawn on in schools in which I myself have worked. Since schools are inevitably relatively closed places, children's experience of the 'real world' tends to be predominantly book based. For this reason the willingness of parents and others to share their experiences with the children provides a real boost to curricular work, often cutting across single subjects to illustrate how knowledge is integrated as it is applied in real life.

Parents as *helpers* in school are also greatly valued by teachers. There are so many necessary jobs to do in preparing and maintaining materials for teaching – covering books, mixing and cleaning paints, making dressing-up clothes, etc. Teachers may quite reasonably feel that their time and expertise should be devoted to teaching as such, rather than to such preparation, and classroom assistants are beyond the means of most schools. A common way of extending this form of help is through the setting up of parental working parties to achieve particular goals such as developing playground equipment or the school environment. On such occasions teams of parents can be found working to provide new facilities for the children of their school.

Parents as participants

In this model parents are once more welcomed into the school but their role is extended from that of a resource provider to that of helping to create learning opportunities. This normally takes place under the supervision of teaching staff and may include such activities as cooking with a small group, running a toy library, reading with some children, going on school visits with the class and supporting children doing craft activities such as sewing, where tangles can be a real problem for individual children.

Parents may thus participate in the work of the school but they remain under the instruction and control of the teacher. Their work is sure to broaden the range of learning experiences made available and is likely to be much appreciated by children and teachers alike. Some forms of training can even be provided for parents who are willing to act in this way. Thus there may be open evenings, workshops or special curriculum-focused events for parents who wish to learn more about teaching and the curriculum so that they can contribute more fully.

Parents can thus make very positive contributions to the work of their children's schools both through providing resources and through active participation in the teachers' work. However, if we follow through the implications of the discussions about learning which have provided a theme for this book, the relationship between teachers and parents needs to go further – into 'partnership'.

Parents as partners

A key issue here concerns the willingness of teachers to share control of the teaching/learning process, to recognize, accept and utilize the knowledge which parents have about their children and to genuinely listen to what parents have to say. This is not easy for teachers to do. Partly it is hard because the parent as client or resource provider has been an established norm for so long. Partly it is difficult simply because it requires more time for talking, discussion and getting to know each other than is normally available.

The value of such forms of partnership are well demonstrated through the work which has been done on children learning to read. Following a number of innovative projects in places such as Rochdale, Bradford, Haringey and Coventry it has now become common practice for teachers to engage in a daily dialogue with parents whilst their children are in the initial stages of reading. Known as 'shared reading' this is often done through a 'going home book' in which teachers and parents exchange comments, record achievements and identify difficulties. It is a means by which they can work *together* towards a specifically defined goal. An example of a page from one such book is provided in Figure 5.2.

At a later stage an interchange might record the beginnings of independent reading (see Figure 5.3). The going home book can also become a vehicle for other types of communication – all of which provide ways of bringing the adults together to support the child. For instance, Figure 5.4 shows an initiative by a worried mother which brings a constructive response from the teacher.

I hope you both enjoy the lovely pictures in this first book.
Miriam and I did enjoy the pictures and we had great fun singing Aunt Rhody. Marvellous — we haven't swung it together yet but obviously we must.

I think Miriam now knows the word <u>and</u>!

She is finding it easier to sit and listen to stories or look at books within the class group now and selects her book very carefully.

The Hare and the Tortoise
"Charley, Charlotte and the Golden Canary" Had to convince Miriam very hard that she really wouldn't like to live at the top flat of a big building like Charlotte.

I love the illustrations in Charley and Charlotte. I'm sure she'll have lots to tell you about the play the teachers did about the turnip.

Figure 5.2 A page from a 'going home book' – early stages of reading

Mr Magnolia – David thought this book was 'a bit silly'.

His ideas and opinions have developed so much, haven't they? He really studies the books so carefully these days – gets absolutely 'lost' in them – it's lovely to see.

King Rollo. We 'had' to read this book six times or more as David really liked it! I thought the stories were very good as each one had a moral to it, but it was written in a way that appeals to children.

Lady Monster and the Bike Ride }
Lady Monster helps out.

He insists that he wants Anthony Rowley but I think 1 or 2 'chapters' will be enough.

We read right through it. The reason he wanted it was that we had seen it beside the tadpoles and toads a few weeks ago. He thought it would be nice to read about them! Sorry if he picked the wrong book, but as he was so keen I encouraged him. The Queen of Hearts

There aren't any wrong books – honestly! I only wondered whether it was quite right for David as it had so much text and so few pictures – it just shows how far his concentration has come if he enjoyed it all. It's very encouraging.

Figure 5.3 A page from a 'going home book' – beginning to read more independently

   Such procedures for partnership are increasingly being developed for mathematical work and in other areas of the curriculum too. After all, if you have the imagination and will to do it, homes can be seen as places where children can really get a rich and wide range of educational experiences. For instance, opportunities for science and maths exist every time meals are cooked, technology is, potentially, part and parcel of many DIY activities, and English is everywhere in our modern, literate environment. From breakfast to bedtime, walking, shopping, making things, cleaning, discussing, playing, eating – opportunities exist for parents to share in and support the learning of their children. In the next few years, it is likely that schools will take increasing steps to involve parents in children's learning and to harness these naturally occurring

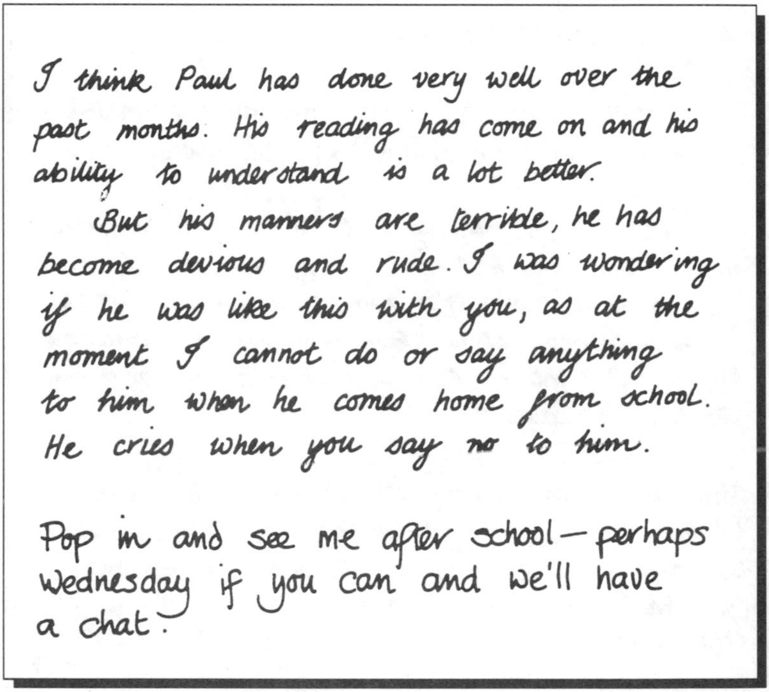

I think Paul has done very well over the past months. His reading has come on and his ability to understand is a lot better.

   But his manners are terrible, he has become devious and rude. I was wondering if he was like this with you, as at the moment I cannot do or say anything to him when he comes home from school. He cries when you say no to him.

Pop in and see me after school – perhaps Wednesday if you can and we'll have a chat.

Figure 5.4   A page from a 'going home book' – broadening the communication

opportunities to the specific goals which are now set by the National Curriculum.

Such school-initiated involvement schemes require careful planning, though. Indeed, they seem to work best when:

- they are clearly focused on a specific curriculum goal;
- a shared teaching approach is discussed, understood and agreed by both teachers and parents;
- the learning process is kept in perspective so that the child is not put under too much pressure.

Of course, such activities still need to be supported by regular discussion and this tends to be easiest to achieve with very young children because it can occur naturally when they are brought to school or collected. With older children, schools which are seriously concerned to develop their partnership with parents regarding children's learning can be distinguished by the lengths they go to set up opportunities for ongoing, focused dialogue between parents and teachers.

Nor should we forget the children in such discussions. As some juniors commented:

'I want to know from my Mum and Dad and the teachers what they think of me ... They should tell me what I've got wrong and right ... what they think of my maths.'

'We should talk all together really because teachers sometimes say things we disagree with and we're never there to say what we think.'

Conclusion

The contribution which parents make to their children's learning is of paramount significance – in subtle, attitudinal ways as well as with regard to explicit knowledge, skills and achievements. Where teachers and parents work in partnership to further children's education, the results are often very impressive. However, such partnership is not easy to achieve and, unfortunately, 'market models' of educational provision seem likely to make it even more difficult.

Suggestions for further reading

For a unique study of the ways in which parents can support the learning of young primary school children, in which extensive case studies of Sally, Daniel, Hazel and other children are offered, see:

> Pollard, A. with Filer, A. (1995) *The Social World of Children's Learning*. London: Cassell.

An important study of parental perspectives on the developments in primary education following the introduction of the National Curriculum is:

> Hughes, M., Wikeley, F. and Nash, T. *Parents and their Children's Schools*. Oxford: Blackwell.

For a practical and lucid introduction to the issues discussed in this chapter, based around an interesting case study of parental involvement in a primary school, see:

> Edwards, V. and Redfern, A. (1988) *At Home in School: Parent Participation in Primary Education*. London: Routledge.

For a collection of articles which provide an overview of the major issue of the 1990s, see:

> Munn, P. (ed.) (1993) *Parents and Schools: Customers, Managers or Partners?* London: Routledge.

The full reference for the latest version of the Government's Parent's Charter is:

> Department for Education (1994) *Our Children's Education: The Updated Parent's Charter*. London: Department for Education.

An excellent research account of the support which parents can offer in early literacy learning is:

> Hannon, P. (1995) *Literacy, Home and School: Research and Practice in Teaching Literacy with Parents*. London: Falmer.

On extending such links more broadly, see:

> David, T. (1993) *Primary Teachers, Parents and Governors*. Stoke-on-Trent: Trentham.

Chapter 6
GOVERNORS, SCHOOL MANAGEMENT AND INSPECTION

Children's understanding can only develop in their own minds, but the circumstances in which they learn are vital. Research has shown that the way schools are run makes a significant difference to children's progress and achievement (Mortimore *et al.*, 1988). In schools, the most relevant factors are the nature of curriculum experiences, the school ethos, the quality of teaching staff and the level and quality of resources. The governors and management of primary schools have a chief responsibility for these factors, although, of course, they themselves must act within the legal and administrative framework set by national and local government. From 1993 new procedures for school inspection were introduced, aiming at a four-year cycle, so that judgements about the quality of provision could be available to parents and others.

In this chapter we begin by considering the powers and responsibilities of governors which were established by the legislation of the late 1980s and early 1990s. The chapter then turns to the role of headteachers and senior staff before focusing on the local management of schools. 'School development plans' are then discussed as a means of providing a sense of strategic purpose through the mass of detail which school management involves. The chapter concludes with an analysis of alternative models of school evaluation and of inspection.

The powers and responsibilities of school governors

The Education Acts 1986, 1988 and 1993 introduced considerable changes in the organization, structure and levels of responsibility within the education service. They contained both centralizing measures which strengthened the power of the Secretary of State, the Department for Education and its agencies, and they introduced decentralizing elements through the new responsibilities vested in school governors for policy formation and headteachers for local management.

The rationale for apparent contradiction between centralism through the Department for Education and decentralization through governing bodies, was that high-quality educational provision would be developed through the creation of a national framework – a structure of safeguards and controls – *within* which there could be relatively high levels of autonomy at school level.

The centralist aspects of the legislative framework became a lived experience for governors and headteachers in the form of an unprecedented flow of circulars and guidelines from the Department for Education, all requiring action in schools. This was particularly the case around the time of the 'review' of the National Curriculum and assessment procedures and seems likely to continue with the new Department for Education and Employment, set up in 1995, the Schools Curriculum and Assessment Authority (SCAA) and Awdurdod Cwricwlwm ac Asesu Cymru (ACAC) in Wales.

However, as we saw in Chapter 5, the Education Reform Act also strengthened the powers of school governors and parents. There were two main contributory factors here. First, there was the thinking, begun in the Taylor Report of 1977, which suggested that parents should have greater representation on the governing bodies of schools because of the contribution which they could make. Second, were the ideas of the Conservative governments of the 1980s that industry and the community should have a greater say in what goes on in education. Such ideas developed into the Education Act 1986 which established a principle of 'balanced interest' on governing bodies between parental, Local Education Authority and 'community' appointees.

Of course, such a redistribution of powers meant, as was its intention, that the influence of Local Education Authorities and of headteachers was weakened. As the government minister of the day put it, power was to be 'shifted from the producers of education to the consumers' and schools were to be enabled to become more responsive to their local communities.

However, it is by no means clear, as yet, that the consumers – parents in particular – actually want the degree of responsibility which goes with the powers and control which they now have the legal right to exercise as governors. Becoming a school governor is now to take on an extremely onerous role. It seems to attract white (98 per cent), middle-aged (60 per cent) men (60 per cent) in professional, management or administrative occupations (60 per cent) and surveys have shown that many governors find the volume and complexity of papers difficult to understand and absorb.

Indeed, the Department for Education and Employment advises that among the powers and duties of governors are to:

- be responsible for the general conduct of the school;
- ensure that the school curriculum is broad and balanced and meets the requirements of the National Curriculum;
- ensure that information about the school, the curriculum and pupil achievement is available to parents;
- offer the headteacher general principles to follow in determining a policy on discipline;
- take part in procedures for selecting school staff and for dismissal or redundancy if necessary, within relevant parts of employment law;
- set a budget for the school and ensures accurate accounts are kept;
- see that the law on religious education and collective worship is complied with;
- decide whether sex education should be provided and, if so, establish a policy to guide provision;
- participate in school inspection procedures and to be responsible for drawing up a post-inspection 'action plan';
- establish a health and safety policy and procedures for monitoring its implementation.

Such responsibilities vary slightly depending on whether the school was established historically by the County Council (a 'maintained' school) or by an independent body. Most commonly the latter are derived from the early provision of education by particular religious denominations. Schools that originated in this way may be 'voluntary aided', in which case their governors retain additional responsibility for religious instruction, admission and maintenance of the site and buildings. Some others are 'voluntary controlled', which means that most of their additional responsibilities have been passed, by agreement, to their Local Education Authority. Governing bodies are to be held accountable too for they must prepare an annual report for parents and hold an annual meeting with parents to discuss the report and any other matters concerning the running of the school.

A particular new duty following the Education Act 1993 is that the governing body of each maintained school must vote on whether to ballot parents to 'opt out' of the system in which funding is provided through their Local Education Authority. The alternative is to apply for 'grant maintained status' (GMS) in which case funding is provided directly from a national Funding Agency for Schools. This policy was heavily promoted by the Conservative government of the early 1990s, with the Secretary of State for Education, John Patten, claiming that such schools offered a 'new freedom' for responding to pupil needs, 'provide a new focus for community life' and 'help bind the community together' (*The Times*, 14 December 1994). Over six million booklets advocating the switch to GMS were printed and distributed to parents by the Department for Education between 1988 and 1994 (*Hansard*, 9 December 1994) and there were regional conferences, videos and advertising campaigns too. However, many parents, governors and teachers associated with primary schools felt that the new type of school status was socially divisive, designed to undermine the existence of locally planned education services and would not enhance the quality of educational provision in their communities as a whole. By the summer of 1994, only 1.8 per cent of English primary schools had become grant maintained (336 schools) and 0.3 per cent of Welsh primary schools (5 schools), and the number of governing bodies voting to proceed to parental ballots slowed to a trickle.

With such important policy issues to consider as well as the practical management and provision of the school, the challenge of being a governor is a very significant one. Indeed, the responsibilities may appear fragmented as well as onerous. However, perhaps, the most helpful way of putting things in perspective is simply to think of the governing body as being responsible for conceiving, securing and maintaining the conditions in which children's learning and development can take place. If this concern with learning and development is highlighted it can begin to provide a means of cutting through the detail, diversity and argument which is likely to arise in most discussion about schools. Governors, immersed in the whirlpool of a late-running meeting, could well take children's learning and development as their touchstone.

Governors, of course, do not face their responsibilities alone and we now turn to consider the roles of the management team in primary schools.

Headteachers and their staff

Management structures within primary schools have changed considerably in recent years. It is now commonplace for headteachers and their deputies to form a close senior management team. They will take the key strategic decisions about how to respond to Department for Education and Employment or Local Education Authority requirements, or to other pressures, and on how to implement the school's plans for future development when it is agreed with governors.

Working closely with them will be a number of staff with 'posts of responsibility', for which they will receive small extra salary allowances. In most schools the allocation of these posts is based on a collegial, team-based model in which each member of staff focuses on, and takes responsibility for, a particular issue or area of the curriculum. For example, there may be posts for maths, English, science, special needs, assessment or home–school links. The staff who develop such expertise are expected to support their colleagues rather like a 'consultant' and to take a lead in developments in their areas.

The quality of primary school management developed a great deal in the late 1980s and early 1990s as new responsibilities were taken on by schools. The administrative and financial aspects of this are discussed below, but the introduction of the National Curriculum was perhaps of even more influence. In particular, the new curriculum framework meant that schools had to be co-ordinated and managed as one entity. Curriculum coherence (across years) and progression (from year to year) could not be provided without considerable planning and co-operation by individual teachers. The result was the development of 'whole-school planning' and the gradual moderation of the classroom autonomy of individual teachers. Further, once the curriculum framework was introduced, processes of pupil assessment, teacher appraisal and whole-school review made it possible for headteachers to identify and pursue issues for development. Indeed, the new structures of accountability to parents and governors ensured that headteachers would act. The overall result has been a 'professionalization' of primary school management. Headteachers are no longer just the 'leading teacher'; they are the managers of all teachers and school resources, and are responsible for the school's external presentation and accountability. Considerable progress has been made, but it has been at a price.

Headteachers have been under enormous pressure in the past few years and it must also be remembered that given the relatively small size of primary schools, many of them have significant teaching loads in addition to all the other demands on their time. Research has confirmed not just the rate of decisions which have to be made, but the enormous variety of them. Within the space of a few moments headteachers commonly move between such things as discussions of school policy, to where to get a supply teacher, who lost a jumper, who hit whom first, whether John is really 'going backwards' as Mrs Jones is suggesting, whether the floors are being cleaned, whether the school can afford more paper and how staff can get appropriate in-service support. Such diversity and pressure can seem remorseless. The relative importance of the issues varies – but they all have to be dealt with.

Furthermore, headteachers tend to feel vulnerable. After all, they have been at the sharp end of a great deal of discussion and legislation for the past decade. The government restricted their autonomy and they had to face public and political criticisms with no appropriate increase in resources or comparable powers of reply. Between 1990–91 and 1993–94 there was a rise of 47 per cent in the number of heads and deputies taking early retirement in England, reaching 1,596 in the later year and affecting 8 per cent of primary schools each year. In the mid-1990s it remained common to find heads who felt that, having come into the profession to 'teach children', they were now left as managers of organizations with externally set goals, limited powers of control and a constant pressure for accountability which prevented them from actually getting on with the job.

One headteacher explained the pleasures and difficulties of the role in the following terms:

> The aspect of the job I value most is the opportunity to work closely with both adults and children – but especially with children. One can theorise brilliantly and plan minutely but the moment of truth lies with child contact ... I particularly remember one young boy who discovered mid-way down a flight of stairs that he could read the note to be taken home to his parents. The exhilaration of the moment made all our efforts worthwhile.
>
> I also value the opportunity to effect change. Headship is not a static, predictable position. Within the routines are a thousand variations of situations. It is both possible and necessary to be a change agent, the bridge between theory and practice.
>
> The aspect of the job I least enjoy is the paperwork ... It would be very easy to get trapped in the office behind great mounds of memos and requests (Marilyn Keerak, cited in Mortimore and Mortimore, 1991, pp. 101–2)

Headteachers have to 'make things work'. They have professional commitments to children but also a practical concern with what it is possible to do in the circumstances they face. They also have a great deal of experience and expertise at the point where education is delivered – in schools.

Local management of schools

One of the most radical aspects of the Education Reform Act 1988 was to increase the autonomy of schools by legislating for local management of schools (LMS). There are two key financial elements in this: 'formula funding' and 'delegation of budgets'.

Formula funding describes the way in which schools are allocated the main part of their income. These formulas are proposed by the Local Education Authority and approved by the Department for Education and Employment. All schools now have control over expenditure through the 'delegation of budgets' from their Local Education Authority and council, to whom initial Community Charge payments and central government grants are paid.

The budget within each Local Education Authority is broken down as described below. The *General Schools Budget* is the total level of financial resources available for all schools in the Local Education Authority. *Mandatory Exceptions* such as capital expenditure, central government training costs of the Local Education Authority advisory or inspection service, must then be provided for and the Local Education Authority will withhold some finance for such purpose. *Discretionary Exceptions*, such as provision of school support services and centres, LEA curriculum development activities, and some building maintenance costs, may also result in up to 10 per cent of the overall General Schools Budget being withheld. The *Aggregated Schools Budget* is the figure which is left and will be by far the greatest sum. It must be allocated directly to schools on the basis of the agreed formula.

The exact basis of formula funding varies between Local Education Authorities but, according to guidelines issued by the Department for Education and Employment, it should:

- be simple;
- be based on the objective needs of schools rather than just continuing previous funding patterns;
- ensure that all schools are treated on an equal basis;
- use the number and age of pupils in each school as the most important factor in the formula.

In fact, Local Education Authority formulas tend to be far from simple and the second criterion above has proved to be too great a challenge to the traditionally greater funding of secondary education. On the latter point a 1994 House of Commons Select Committee report again emphasized the importance of achieving greater parity in funding across the two phases. Notwithstanding this major issue, the great diversity in the circumstances of all schools has meant that the whole funding issue has proved to be much more complex than was initially appreciated. For instance, socio-economic and cultural variations are enormous across the country so the community needs which schools must meet differ greatly. Similarly schools vary a lot in terms of their actual costs, e.g. because of teachers at different stages of their careers or differences in the age and construction of buildings, and so on. Trials for a national funding scheme using a 'Common Funding Formula' began in 1994 but, so far, seem unlikely to overcome the complexities which must be faced.

The most important element of the formula in all Local Education Authorities is the number of pupils on the school's roll. Audits of such numbers are taken termly and converted into units of funding based on the age of each pupil, known as 'age weighted pupil units' (AWPU). In primary schools the AWPU for most children was worth about £1,000 in 1994 and it can be seen that any significant variability in the pupil enrolment at a school would have a rapid effect on the budget. This is the power behind the 'market model' of education. Even where schools oppose the competitive model on which it is based, they remain subject to its strictures.

The implications of local management of schools are thus likely to raise thorny problems for headteachers and governing bodies for many years. The opportunities for local decision-making are very much welcomed but the inadequacy and instability of funding is a large problem for many schools, particularly where they are exposed to market forces which they cannot control, such as in inner-city locations.

However, some constructive ways of producing curriculum-led, as opposed to finance-led, management have also been introduced and it is to these which we now turn.

School development plans

Governors and senior staff in schools have an excellent means of reviewing, evaluating and planning the work of the school as a whole through the use of 'school development plans'. These documents can provide a focus for the self-evaluative work of school staffs and provide a vehicle for strategic planning by the senior management, teachers and governors. As Hargreaves and Hopkins (1991) argued, the potential is to produce 'the empowered school' through structured participation, reflection and planning. The use of school development planning has been monitored by HMI and its role in bringing about school improvement was endorsed in a 1994 report by the Office for Standards in Education (OFSTED). In particular, they pointed out the combined role of 'careful rational planning and the commitment of teachers, heads, pupils and governors' (OFSTED, 1994, p. 7).

A school development plan is the product of a great deal of discussion, thought and planning. The procedure starts with a recognition and acceptance of legal requirements and constraints, but it then moves directly to an analysis, or 'audit', of the specific needs of the particular school. At this point negotiation with a wide range of people, including staff, parents and governors may be undertaken. From this initial analysis of needs, a school development plan is constructed.

School development plans vary in their precise content in different Local Education Authorities but they are likely to contain statements relating to:

1. The school's aims and philosophy.
2. The school's present situation:
   catchment
   organization
   staffing
   curriculum provision

resources
achievements.
3. Assessed needs for future development:
   organizational development targets
   staff development targets
   curriculum development targets
   resource development targets.
4. Action plans of how the assessed needs are to be met.

The fourth point is a key one for school development and for ensuring that the quality of educational provision keeps on rising. It takes the focus to the stage of implementation which is where the teachers and other staff of the school will be particularly important. This process has been represented as a cycle by Hargreaves and Hopkins (1991) and this is shown in Figure 6.1.

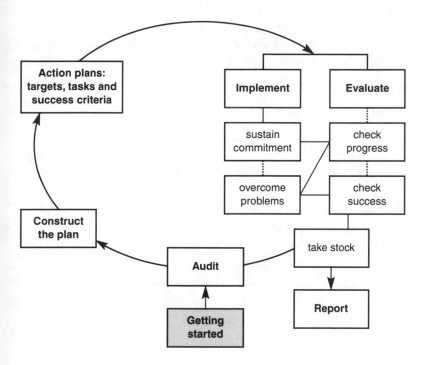

Figure 6.1 The development planning process

Perhaps the most important question remains; 'how do we judge how much progress is being made?' There have been two basic answers to this question of evaluation. First, through attempts at local self-assessment, using the development planning process with the support of Local Education Authority advisors or inspectors and, second, following the Education (Schools) Act of 1992, through the external inspection of schools in a national programme.

Self-evaluation of school performance

This approach was elaborated in the early 1990s following the endorsement by most Local Education Authorities of school development planning. It is particularly appropriate for formative, ongoing development work and is reflected in Figure 6.1

As part of the process, when specific targets for development have been identified, it is recommended that 'success criteria' are drawn up. These should be relatively objective and can be used to evaluate the school's achievements at the end of the year. For instance, the Audit Commission offered advice on this in 1991 and provided the illustration of 'success criteria' in Table 6.1.

Table 6.1 An illustration of aims with explicit success criteria (Audit Commission, 1991)

Aim	Success criteria
To acquire abilities, knowledge and the will to use them	Monitoring and recording of skills and pupils' achievement
To read fluently and accurately, with understanding, feeling and discrimination	Tests and other assessments of accurate reading ability
To encourage pupils to enjoy books	Number of books issued from school library Pupils to keep records of books read

The essence of this model is that there is an emphasis on self-improvement. There is thus a strong attempt to support teachers and governors in evaluating their own performance prior to restarting the annual planning cycle again. Local authority advisers, where they exist, have been particularly important in providing support for this since they provide an external eye and comparative experience from the many schools with which they are familiar.

As an example of the way this process can work we can imagine a school where consultations reveal a concern about children's ability to co-operate and solve problems together. As well as being an excellent means of learning and understanding in its own right (see Chapter 4), this issue is raised in many places in National Curriculum documentation. When the staff and governors meet to draw up the school development plan they would thus identify the specific target of improving co-operative problem-solving. They would now have to think both of ways of developing towards the goal and of success criteria which would be appropriate for assessing progress.

Identifying success criteria is by no means easy. They must be easily understood, appropriate to the target and practical to evaluate. Additionally, a secure basis for evaluation can only really be provided if one has information about the situation at the start of a programme of development (input data), information on how things are developed (process data) and information on the results (output data). To assess performance we thus need information to monitor school performance (see Figure 6.2).

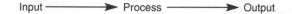

Input ⎯⎯⎯⎯⎯⟶ Process ⎯⎯⎯⎯⎯⟶ Output

Figure 6.2 Information stages for monitoring school performance

Some data may be relatively 'objective' – numbers of children, budgets for in-service training of staff, etc. Other sorts of important data are likely to be relatively 'subjective' – judgements about childrens' self-confidence, interpersonal skills, the divergence of their ideas, etc. Both sorts of data are valuable and necessary and it is important to avoid reducing the evidence considered to just that which is measurable. After all, many of the most important things in education are not directly measurable. For factors such as these, there is no substitute for the professional judgement of experienced and appropriately trained teachers.

In our example of co-operative problem-solving, we might take success criteria for the 'process stage' as being:

- acquisition of resources suitable for co-operative problem-solving;
- revision of curriculum policy documents to explore opportunities for increasing co-operative problem-solving activities;
- staff development programmes focused on managing co-operative problem solving activities in classrooms;
- a rising number of classroom sessions in which co-operative problem-solving is a central part of a task.

At the 'output stage' school staff may consider:

- the quality of talking, listening and respect for others shown by children in group situations;
- the nature and quality of children's learning achievements through group work.

Where adopted effectively, such developmental procedures are a powerful way of engendering self-reflection and internally generated improvement in a school. However, further measures for monitoring the quality of schooling have also been developed in the 1990s.

The national inspection of school performance

As we have seen, one powerful theme running through the Education Reform Act 1988 concerned accountability and the need to provide evidence of educational standards for parents and others. The procedures for pupil assessment at ages 7, 11, 14 and 16 provide one sort of information and the Department for Education and Employment also collects other quantitative data which is indicative of school and Local Education Authority performance.

However, the Government decided to introduce a new form of national inspection and this was initiated by OFSTED in September 1993. National inspection is a 'top-down' model in which centrally defined criteria for performance and processes for inspection are set out in a *Framework for Inspection* document. Teams of inspectors, led by a Registered Inspector and including an inspector with a non-educational background, then negotiate with OFSTED for a contract to inspect particular schools. From these schools, they require extensive advance documentation and they then visit schools for up to one week with a team, for primary schools, of between three and six inspectors. They study documents, talk to teachers, pupils, parents, governors and the senior staff and make extensive observations of lessons. The quality of classroom practice is

Criteria for inspection are nationally defined

↓

Evidence to be collected is nationally defined

↓

School inspection is organized by OFSTED

↓

Inspection takes place

↓

A public report is produced by the Registered Inspector

↓

An Action Plan is produced by the Governing Body

↓

The Action Plan is enacted by school staff

Figure 6.3 A 'top-down' model of school inspection as used by OFSTED

recorded on a scale from very good, good, satisfactory, unsatisfactory and poor. Finally, the Registered Inspector writes a report reflecting the inspectors' judgement on:

- educational standards;
- quality of education;
- efficiency of resource management;
- the spiritual, moral, social and cultural development of pupils.

Once issued, this report must be made publicly available and a summary sent to parents. Governors are then required, within 40 days of receiving the report, to draw up an 'action plan' setting out steps which it is intended to take to remedy any weaknesses which have been identified.

Comprehensive advice to schools is provided in the form of a 'handbook' (OFSTED, 1995), a publication which sold over 55,000 copies in its first year of publication, 1993. The model then, is as shown in Figure 6.3.

There have been a number of practical difficulties with the implementation of this form of inspection. For instance, there was initially an inadequate number of trained inspectors willing to inspect the approximately 18,000 primary schools in England and Wales and, even with further recruitment, OFSTED may be unable to provide the intended four-year cycle of inspection for all schools. The style of the written reports has been criticized for being depersonalized, passive, boring and inaccessible to parents. The criteria by which schools are assessed and the reliability of the judgements made by inspectors have been subjected to critique by researchers. Teacher associations have also been unenthusiastic with the National Union of Teachers conducting a survey which faulted the poor preparation of the 'mostly male, white inspectors' and suggested that some were: 'poking around in cupboards, not reading the documentation properly, applying the criteria poorly, displaying bias and a lack of sensitivity towards teachers' (reported in *Education*, 22 July 1994).

It is perhaps not surprising that teachers are nervous and sometimes worried by the nature of the national inspection system. It is externally imposed and they have no sense of ownership of it. Criteria are set by OFSTED and may not reflect the priorities of the school. Inspection outcomes are immediately placed in the public domain, yet schools have little redress if they dispute a judgement or conclusion.

Such a system may produce fear, as it did in a previous manifestation in Victorian times, but it is uncertain that such a top-down model can provide a strong dynamic for learning and development coming from *within* the school. Indeed, many headteachers, whilst accepting the need to evaluate their school's performance and to be held accountable, fear that the externally imposed mechanistic way in which inspection processes have been set up fails to represent, or could even actually damage, the essence of what they are really trying to achieve in terms of children's learning, self-confidence and quality of experience at school.

Some feel that the national inspection system is focused on various aspects of teaching, school policies and structures, rather than on learning and the quality of pupil experience. As a former HMI and OFSTED inspector wrote, commenting on the initial *Handbook for Inspection of Schools*: 'Nowhere is the idea that one of the major roles of senior staff is to know what the child actually experiences', whilst school management becomes: 'mere administrative flummery, concerned with the maintenance of a structure but not the learning of pupils' (Christopher Bowring-Carr, *Education*, 11 November 1994).

This last point is important for there is a possibility that the 'high-stakes' nature of national inspection will undermine the effectiveness of continuous self-directed programmes of school improvement. Will these be seen as a side-show? Will locally determined priorities and aims become subjugated to those which are set nationally? Through what processes should schools be held accountable?

Conclusion

Governors, parents and teachers face difficult challenges in education and they need the firm and constant support of each other, together with a spirit of openness and commitment. The nature of management in primary schools has developed considerably in recent years, particularly following the introduction of the National Curriculum and various accountability requirements. Maximizing the quality of children's learning opportunities is a far from easy job and it is one which, in the long term, can only be accomplished collaboratively. National inspection procedures of the early 1990s could helpfully be revised so that they *complement*, rather than distort, more continuous processes of locally responsive, whole-school development.

Suggestions for further reading

A comprehensive guide to the role of a school governor remains:
> Wragg, E.C. and Partington, J.A. (1995) *The School Governors' Handbook* (3rd edn). London: Routledge.

See also:
> Sallis, J. (1994) *Heads and Governors: Building the Partnership*. London: Routledge.

For legal advice, the Department for Education and Employment provides a guide which, in recent years, has been updated annually:
> Department for Education (1994) *School Governors: A Guide to the Law*. London: Department for Education.

There are many books on school management, most of which are written for teachers. Among the more accessible and practical is:
> Pountney, G. (1993) *Primary School Management*. London: Cassell.

The experience of being a headteacher after the Education Reform Act 1988 is captured through the case-studies in:
> Mortimore, P. and Mortimore, J. (1991) *The Primary Head: Roles, Responsibilities and Reflections*. London: Chapman.

The best study of the collaborative culture which is often to be found among primary school staff is:
> Nias, J., Southworth, G. and Yeomans, R. (1989) *Staff Relationships in the Primary School*. London: Cassell.

For influential text, on how to develop self-management in schools and on school development planning see:

Caldwell, B. and Spinks, J. (1988) *The Self-Managing School*. London: Falmer.

Hargreaves, D. and Hopkins, D. (1991) *The Empowered School*. London: Cassell.

The key document on primary school inspection is:

OFSTED (1995) *Handbook: Guidance on the Inspection of Nursery and Primary Schools*. London: OFSTED.

However, for a riposte to top-down models, see:

Fullan, M. and Hargreaves, A. (1992) *What's Worth Fighting for in Your School? Working Together for Improvement*. Milton Keynes: Open University Press.

Chapter 7
FUTURE CHALLENGES

Education is still adapting to the biggest challenge this century which came with the Education Reform Act 1988. The National Curriculum and the new ways of managing schools and teachers were explicitly intended to increase educational 'standards' and the quality of children's education. However, it remains by no means certain that they will succeed – indeed, the search for improved standards of education is historically comparable to that for the Holy Grail. In ten years' time we may still be looking for it! In the case of education though, the reason for the constant search is usually that we change our minds about what, precisely, we are looking for.

In any event, as we move to the millennium we will all have the opportunity to test the propositions and goals which are now enshrined in legislation. The National Curriculum and assessment procedures are now part of our children's lives and the test of them is thus directly empirical. Its effects should be visible to every family with young children and to every adult who takes the time to become involved in the life of a school. For our children's sake, we must all sincerely hope that the new structures will be a success and, in general terms, the challenge of the future is to ensure that this is the case.

However, it would be naive and irresponsible to leave the discussion there, because there are a number of potential difficulties which must be addressed if we are to make progress. In this brief concluding chapter, I therefore want to raise a few of the most important challenges which we face – challenges which we must overcome if we are to make progress and challenges which we can only overcome if parents, governors and teachers collaborate together.

As a vehicle for this, and to reassert the point that children themselves ultimately control their own learning, we can return to the case with which I began this book – to Naomi and her new shoes.

Naomi's note

She wrote:

> I'm happy, I'm happy,
> I know I am. I'm sure I am,
> I'm happy because I got new shoes.

Thinking of Naomi here is important because her simple message conveys some of the realities of children learning – the qualities of openness and immediacy, the links between children's development, experience and growing competence, the importance of trusting relationships between adults and children. If we are really concerned about learning, these are things which matter enormously. Curriculum attainment targets, assessment procedures, local management of schools, national inspection and all the rest, may be important – but they are simply adjuncts of the learning process. They should be in its service – supporting, facilitating, enabling – as each child gradually constructs his or her understanding of the world. The danger is that they may become an encumbrance, a set of diversions and a framework of constraints which have little resonance with children's immediate needs. Indeed, the legislation of the late 1980s and early 1990s could produce bureaucratic 'clutter' which would be really very damaging. I will consider some of the challenges which are now posed.

Programmes of study and the quality of pupil experience

Taken as a whole, the specification of programmes of study in the revised National Curriculum must be a positive advance. It will ensure breadth of experience and should also provide progression with less risk of overload in its revised, post-1995 form. However, there remains a danger that programmes of study could become a strait-jacket, for there is now evidence that much of children's learning does not proceed in a generalizable, linear way. Ultimately, each child will learn in his or her own way, through a self-constructed route to understanding.

True, it is important that adults provide suitable instruction and a supportive structure, but we have to be very careful that this does not become a conveyor belt which processes children and from which no one can escape. If the potential richness, variety and excitement of the curriculum becomes reduced to moving from work-task to work-task then we will have failed our children. In this context, we should very much fear the results of the massive plans by some publishers to produce 'work schemes' for the subjects specified by the National Curriculum.

Assessment and children's learning

Assessment can be seen as being at the centre of the learning process. When it is devoted to that end, with an emphasis on ongoing, formative, teacher assessment, its development is likely to be a considerable help in developing the quality of understanding of children and of what is provided for them. However, assessment could also become a diversionary pressure, an intrusion and a threat.

It could be a diversionary pressure if it comes to take up such a large proportion of teacher time that teachers have little scope for other important aspects of their role. We know that this has happened in parts of the USA so it is a real concern. Should Naomi's teacher have recorded the detail of her emerging competence at writing or should she have talked to her or written back?

Assessment could become an intrusion if it begins to sour relationships between children and teachers. Children, being clever and canny, will know what is going on and will be aware when teachers are forming judgements about them. Given that the basis of close relationships must be trust and a mutual exchange of dignity, the assessment process could thus easily compromise the whole quality of classroom experience for both children and teachers. Since this has been one of the great strengths of primary education over many years, it must not be allowed to happen – Naomi wrote because she wanted to share her excitement with her teacher.

Assessment could become a threat because of the possible use and consequences of reported results. It is naive to pretend that children will not soon know of the 'levels of attainment' which have been attributed to them – just ask any infant school child to compare how they are getting on at reading with the progress of one of their friends. The result, for some children, must inevitably be a sense of relative failure and a loss of self-esteem. There is also a very real danger of social stigma. How would public reporting of results have affected Naomi and her classmates? In addition, public reporting through league tables remains a considerable worry. The damage to school stability if market forces act on enrolments could be considerable.

Assessment procedures are thus very powerful. They could do a lot of good, but they could be very damaging too. Given the delicacy and interpersonal subtlety of many learning processes in classrooms, assessment will have to be handled with extreme care. Given the market conditions into which schools have been placed, crude interpretation of assessment data could be catastrophic for particular schools.

Teacher professionalism

How the new educational structures are interpreted and enacted will depend on professional judgement, skill, knowledge and commitment. The profession shows many strengths, and some weaknesses. For instance, there is a considerable body of research evidence which demonstrates the sophistication of teachers' thinking, the ways in which judgement is exercised and the skills which are developed. And yet, many of these judgements and skills seem to be primarily focused on managing classrooms from the control point of view rather than on children's learning *per se*. Similarly, the actual subject knowledge of many primary teachers is a little shaky in some areas, such as science and technology, and this inevitably causes some difficulties in interpreting the challenge of learning tasks and in diagnosing each child's needs. It is clear then, that support and help for teachers as they develop their professional expertise must be provided.

This will not be easy if we have a shortage of teachers and if morale is depressed by constant criticism as it was in the early 1990s. However, teachers derive great personal satisfaction from their work with children and are likely to respond positively if their work is respected and valued appropriately. Naomi trusted and valued her teacher – it is not a great deal to ask that other people should do so too.

Local management of schools

Control of the greater part of a school's budget has brought considerable autonomy to governors and headteachers and, this greater budgetary control has enabled schools to match their specific needs against expenditure with more precision than in the past.

Local management of schools is a main administrative pressure, however, and there is growing evidence that it is diverting headteachers from their primary responsibility for the children's learning. To lead their staff team effectively, headteachers need to stay in touch, to teach some of the time, retain their curricular expertise, and to have time to talk to people.

'Management by wandering about' is not sufficient for a headteacher in the 1990s, but it does remain necessary for the person-centred environments which schools are. Like Naomi, her teacher also has need of praise, encouragement and guidance and this could not happen if her headteacher was buried under computer printouts, or worrying about school marketing or maintenance in her office. It thus remains to be seen if some administrative services would be more effectively co-ordinated centrally by local, regional or even national bodies.

Resources for learning

The devolution of budgetary control to schools says nothing about the absolute level of the funding which is provided and one of the biggest challenges for the millennium is undoubtedly that of increasing resources for primary education. The present imbalance between primary, secondary and tertiary education reflects historical precedent rather than any real appreciation of what it would really cost to meet the needs of young children.

Since the introduction of the National Curriculum, teachers in primary schools have been under simply enormous pressure and the resources available to them are totally unrealistic. In particular, in addition to the actual process of teaching, they need more time to liaise, plan, prepare, monitor, record, report and discuss regarding the children's learning. With present proportions of contact time with children, the work which teachers are now being asked to do will remain impossible.

The most positive way forward is to move to a system of 'activity-led' staffing, in which the time needed to do the job is calculated and then provided. This would cost significant sums of money and it will need a sustained campaign to provide it. If it is not forthcoming, the Naomi's of the future may discover that their teacher hardly has time to read their notes, let alone reply.

Equal opportunities

For many years, people in the education service have consciously worked to provide equality of educational opportunity for all children. However, given the seeming intractability of the conditions and social relationships which give rise to social differences, most people would recognize that enormous scope for improvement with regard to gender, ethnicity, social class and disability remain. The 'Recommendation' from the Council of Europe (1985), on *Teaching and Learning about Human Rights in Primary Schools*, reinforces this point and draws on the European Convention of Human Rights. Equal opportunities thus remains a very important concern. However, there is now considerable evidence that inequalities have been growing in the UK in recent years. The poorest families are now in very difficult circumstances.

Unfortunately, some provisions of the Education Reform Act 1988 and the Education Act of 1993, seem likely to increase inequalities, particularly in provision between schools. This essentially arises because of the choice of the market mechanism as a means of improving educational standards. To make a market operate, there needs to be both information and choice. With regard to schools, information is to be provided by the publication of assessment results, of school brochures, inspection reports and through annual meetings for parents. To achieve choice there is the 'open enrolment' policy which requires schools to admit pupils on demand up to their Planned Admission Level. The resourcing of schools is then to be largely based on the numbers of pupils attending (see Chapter 6). Popular schools should thus flourish and less popular schools will, so the theory goes, have to consider the reasons for their difficulties and improve.

Perhaps this might work if all 'reasons' for differences in levels of performance were under the control of schools, if the practicalities of family life made it possible for all parents to send their children anywhere and if no parent ever made judgements about the work of schools for educationally unsound reasons. However, none of these conditions can realistically be satisfied. The result is that the consequences of the use of market mechanism could be very damaging and this is becoming particularly apparent in inner-city schools. Children's entitlement – their right to a high level of provision whichever school they attend – is at risk. Indeed, it is likely that social divisions of ethnicity, as well as social class, will be reinforced by this reliance on market forces.

I would suggest that Naomi, and her generation, will not be best served for their future, or for their contribution to our development in the next century, by the continued reinforcement of the unjustifiable indignities of the British social class system which seems to be occurring. However, how to balance the individual rights and responsibilities of parents regarding their children with wider social, economic and ethical imperatives remains the prime duty of government. It is thus to future governments which we must look if the fears which I have expressed above do materialize – and, of course, it is for us to elect and influence governments.

Conclusion

Despite concerns such as those outlined above, and perhaps because of them, we owe it to our children to think, co-operate and act constructively. I believe that we must face national educational structures and requirements constructively, must monitor and address any weaknesses in schools as they emerge, and must support teachers in developing their professionalism. We must secure appropriate funding for primary education. We can only realistically succeed in these challenges by taking new opportunities which are open to us and by sharing and drawing together in a collaborative spirit.

Above all though, we need the resolution and determination to work positively to develop the learning and learning experiences of all young children. Through this collective endeavour, parents, governors and teachers can each play large parts in constructing our future.

Part Two
RESOURCES FOR
UNDERSTANDING
PRIMARY EDUCATION

Chapter 8

INFLUENCES, ISSUES AND CONCEPTS FOR PRIMARY EDUCATION: A COMPENDIUM

This compendium has been designed to provide a simple and accessible resource for reference purposes when new names, terms, issues or references are encountered. It has been organized in terms of *influences*, *issues* and *concepts*, with clusters of related terms being defined and explained in a logical juxtaposition.

The clusters of topics covered by this structure are indicated in Figure 8.1. In general, those identified as *influences* constitute and create the contexts in which primary education takes place. Within this, classroom practice can be described in terms of three, interrelated 'message systems' of curriculum, pedagogy and assessment (see Bernstein, 1975; Pollard *et al.*, 1994 for illustrative research). In addition, there are many *issues* and *concepts* which are associated with social processes and consequences in primary schools.

All of the specific items covered in this compendium can be accessed through the alphabetical index. Many are also cross-referenced to their use in earlier chapters.

Purposes and historical influences

Aims

General statements about the overall purposes of educational provision which are set at national, local, school and classroom levels or even for particular pupils (see Chapter 3). Clarity in aims is particularly useful for the planning and evaluation of practice (see Chapter 6, p. 114).

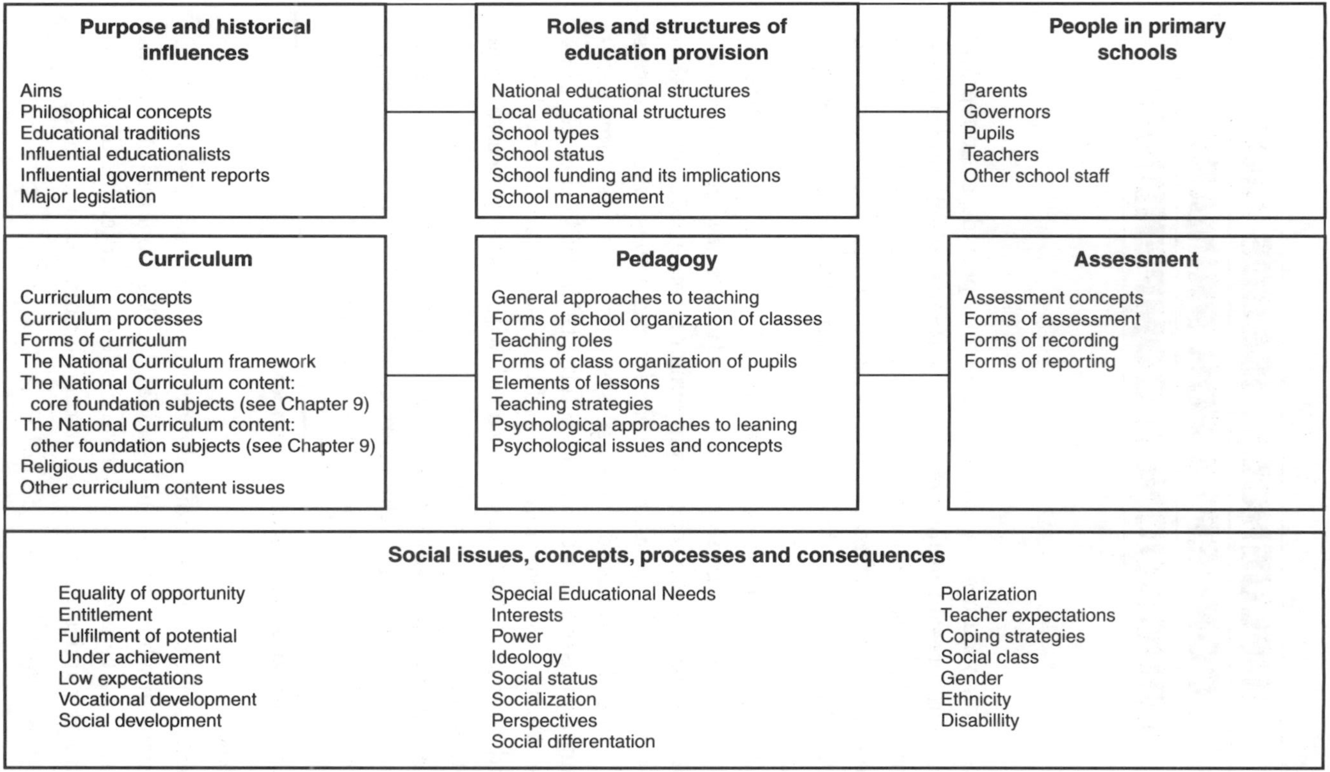

Purpose and historical influences

Aims
Philosophical concepts
Educational traditions
Influential educationalists
Influential government reports
Major legislation

Roles and structures of education provision

National educational structures
Local educational structures
School types
School status
School funding and its implications
School management

People in primary schools

Parents
Governors
Pupils
Teachers
Other school staff

Curriculum

Curriculum concepts
Curriculum processes
Forms of curriculum
The National Curriculum framework
The National Curriculum content:
  core foundation subjects (see Chapter 9)
The National Curriculum content:
  other foundation subjects (see Chapter 9)
Religious education
Other curriculum content issues

Pedagogy

General approaches to teaching
Forms of school organization of classes
Teaching roles
Forms of class organization of pupils
Elements of lessons
Teaching strategies
Psychological approaches to leaning
Psychological issues and concepts

Assessment

Assessment concepts
Forms of assessment
Forms of recording
Forms of reporting

Social issues, concepts, processes and consequences

Equality of opportunity
Entitlement
Fulfilment of potential
Under achievement
Low expectations
Vocational development
Social development

Special Educational Needs
Interests
Power
Ideology
Social status
Socialization
Perspectives
Social differentiation

Polarization
Teacher expectations
Coping strategies
Social class
Gender
Ethnicity
Disability

Figure 8.1 Influences, issues and concepts in the compendium on primary education

Philosophical concepts

Needs   A value judgement made about an educational priority, often in respect of 'what children need'.

Interests   A term often used in respect of children to denote topics or activities which they are thought to find attractive and around which a curriculum might be constructed. Also used to highlight the status, values or financial concerns of those involved in political struggles, for instance between teachers and Conservative pressure groups in the late 1980s (see Chapter 3, p. 35).

Rights   Entitlements to *receive* opportunities from others. For instance, of children in respect of the National Curriculum from schools, parents in respect of high-quality schools from governors and Local Education Authorities and teachers in respect of sound national and local education policies, structures and resources (e.g., see Chapter 5, p. 93).

Responsibilities   Obligations to *provide* opportunities to others. For instance, of schools to provide an appropriate curriculum, including the National Curriculum, to children, of parents to support teachers in their work for their children and of national and local government to provide sound national education policies, structures and resources (e.g., see Chapter 5, p. 90 and Chapter 6, p. 109).

Educational traditions

The elementary tradition   A form of educational practice and provision associated with the mass education of the nineteenth century with a narrow concentration on the 3Rs (reading, 'riting and 'rithmetic) and with authoritarian discipline.

The developmental tradition   A form of educational practice and provision which emphasizes the ways in which children develop physically, socially, emotionally and intellectually as a basis for planning and organizing learning.

The preparatory tradition A form of practice and provision which sees primary education as a 'preparation' for secondary education and which has been particularly influential in the independent school sector where children are examined prior to acceptance in 'public schools' (independent secondary schools).

Influential educationalists

Froebel, F. (1782–1852) Founder of Kindergarten system in Germany who emphasized respect for the autonomy of young children and the importance of structured play. Influential in nursery and infant school education.

Montessori, Maria (1870–1952) Italian educator who believed that 'play is the child's work' and that a sequence of child development could be structured through a series of planned play activities using specific equipment. Particularly influential in nursery education within the independent sector.

Piaget, Jean (1896–1980) Swiss psychologist who, through his studies of child development, identified four 'stages': sensori-motor, pre-operational, concrete operations and formal operations through which children pass in a developmental process as they adapt to and assimilate their environment. His work was interpreted as legitimating the 'child-centred' ideas which were very influential in primary education in the late 1960s and 1970s. The most influential 'constructivist' psychologist (see Chapter 1, p. 10).

Skinner, B. F. (b. 1904) American psychologist who, through his studies of animal behaviour, identified the ways in which learning can be affected by chains of conditioning between 'stimuli' and 'response'. Such 'behaviourist' work provides a rationale for 'rote' learning, practice and some forms of skill development (see Chapter 1, p. 10).

Gagné, Robert (b. 1916) A behaviourist psychologist whose work established the concept of staged 'hierarchies of learning', an idea that underpins the many mathematics and other published 'schemes' used in primary schools.

Bruner, Jerome (b. 1915) American psychologist, much influenced by Vygotsky, who demonstrated the modern relevance of his work. A proponent of a 'cultural psychology' in which social aspects of learning are taken very seriously (see Chapter 1, p. 11).

Vygotsky, L. S. (1891–1934) Russian psychologist who analysed the importance of social context and interaction in learning. His most influential concept is the 'zone of proximal development'. The most influential 'social constructivist' psychologist (see Chapter 1, p. 11).

Stenhouse, Lawrence (1926–1982) British educator who demonstrated how teachers can 'research' on their own classroom practice and thus improve the quality of their provision. Associated with 'action research', 'reflective practice' and 'continuing professional development'.

Influential government reports

The Hadow Report (1931) *The Primary School*, was an influential official expression of 'progressive' ideas. The most quoted assertion is, 'The curriculum is to be thought of in terms of activity and experience rather than knowledge to be acquired and facts to be stored'.

The Plowden Report (1967) *Children and their Primary Schools*, promoted the applications of developmental psychology (particularly from Piaget) in primary school teaching and has been regarded as an important influence on 'progressive' and 'child-centred' ideas which were popular among teachers in the late 1960s and 1970s (see Chapter 4, p. 63).

The Bullock Report (1975) *A Language for Life*, argued that children's language is of paramount importance and should be developed *across* the whole curriculum through systematic school policies.

The Warnock Report (1978) *Special Education: Forward Trends*, established that one in five children have special educational needs at some point in their school education and needed particular provision. The Education Act 1981 enacted many of the report's recommendations including an emphasis on the integration of children with SEN and the issue of 'statements' of pupil need.

The Cockcroft Report (1982) *Mathematics Counts*, set out the arguments for the importance of mathematics in everyday life and advocated innovative teaching methods including problem-solving and the use of calculators and computers.

The Elton Report (1989) *Discipline in Schools*, a balanced account which documented how 'most schools are well ordered', also the cumulative impact of 'minor disruption'. It suggested that teacher status and training could be enhanced; highlighted the importance of school effective management and parental guidance; and emphasized the role of pupils taking responsibility.

The House of Commons Select Committee Report (1986) *Achievement in Primary Schools*, provided a thorough overview of the state of primary education in the mid-1980s. Among its recommendations was the suggestion that class teachers should also act as 'curriculum co-ordinators' for particular subjects across the whole school (see Chapter 6, p. 110).

The House of Commons Select Committee Report (1994) *The Disparity in Funding between Primary and Secondary Schools*, concluded that the gap in funding between the two sectors was too wide, with expenditure on secondary pupils being more than 40 per cent higher than on primary pupils, despite the range of new demands made following the introduction of the National Curriculum. Concerns about rising class sizes were expressed.

Main legislation

Education Act 1870   Established 'elementary schools' to fill the gaps in the previously voluntary provision of education for young children.

Education Act 1944   Abolished elementary schools and established 'primary schools'. It also enabled remaining voluntary schools to change their status to 'aided' or 'controlled' and receive state funding within one national system of primary education. In secondary education, it established grammar, secondary modern and technical schools (see Chapter 3, p. 41).

Education Act 1981   Enacted most of the recommendations of the Warnock Report on provision for children with special educational needs. It required that children with SEN be issued with a 'statement' of those needs and encouraged the integration of children with SEN within mainstream provision.

Education Act 1986   Established governing bodies for each school with a specific composition and set of powers for each school size and status. Set a requirement for governing bodies to adopt a curriculum policy, and to provide an annual school report and annual meeting for parents (see Chapter 6, p. 107).

Teachers' Pay and Conditions Act 1987   Abolished teacher's rights to independent negotiating procedures over pay and working conditions and authorized the Secretary of State to impose pay and conditions. He or she is advised by a School Teachers' Review Body.

Education Reform Act 1988   Set national educational aims for the first time and established the National Curriculum and a body to oversee it (The National Curriculum Council, NCC – abolished 1993); national assessment requirements and a body to oversee them (The School Examination and Assessment Council, SEAC – abolished 1993); requirements for the provision of information to parents; a policy of 'open enrolment' and parental choice of school; delegation of finances from Local Education Authorities to schools; and the opportunity for large primary schools to 'opt out' of Local Education Authority control and become 'grant maintained' (GMS) (see Chapter 3, p. 40 and Chapter 6, p. 109).

Children Act 1989   Wide-ranging legislation which sought to establish a comprehensive framework for the co-ordination of all forms of law, service and support for children. The Act increased parental powers and those of the courts whilst also emphasizing children's rights. Procedures for the work of professionals and agencies are complex.

Education (Schools) Act 1992   Established new procedures for the inspection of schools by 'Registered Inspectors' on a regular cycle (planned to be every four years) and to be co-ordinated by the Office for Standards in Education (OFSTED). Though led by the Chief Inspector of Schools and supported by Her Majesty's Inspectors, the number of HMI was reduced and the system was introduced in which inspection is conducted by independent teams working to contract (see Chapter 6, p. 119).

Education Act 1993   Set up the Funding Agency for Schools (FAS) to administer funding for grant maintained schools (GMS) after opt out from Local Education Authority control. Specified procedures for opting out and regulations for the governance of GMS. Additionally established a 'Code of Practice' for national structuring of provision of special educational needs. Introduced regulations for monitoring school attendance and procedures for the identification and monitoring of schools which are 'failing to provide an acceptable standard of education' (see Chapter 6, p. 109).

Sex Discrimination Act 1976   Prohibited sex discrimination in school admissions, teacher appointments and curricular and other provision.

Race Relations Act 1976   Prohibited discrimination on grounds of ethnicity in school admissions, teacher appointments and curricular and other provision.

Roles and structures of educational provision

National educational roles and structures

The Secretary of State for Education   The chief minister of national government with responsibility for national education policy. Appointed by the Prime Minister and a cabinet post.

The Department for Education and Employment (DfEE)   The national government department with responsibility for education.

The Office for Standards in Education (OFSTED)   A national government body set up in 1993 which appoints and trains school inspectors, arranges and sets criteria for school inspection processes and produces public reports on individual schools and on the national system more generally (see Chapter 6, p. 119).

Her Majesty's Inspectors of schools (HMI)   A small group of professional inspectors of schools now working with OFSTED but with a tradition, since 1839, of providing independent advice on the education system (see Chapter 6, p. 119).

The School Curriculum and Assessment Authority (SCAA) The national government agency set up in 1993 and responsible for implementation, evaluation and advice regarding the National Curriculum and assessment procedures in England (see Chapter 3, p. 42).

Awdurdod Cwricwlwm ac Asesu Cymru (Curriculum and Assessment Authority of Wales) (ACAC)   A national government agency set up in 1993 and responsible for implementation, evaluation and advice regarding the National Curriculum and assessment procedures in Wales (see Chapter 3, p. 42).

The Funding Agency for Schools (FAS)   A national body set up in 1993 to disburse funds to Grant Maintained Schools (see Chapter 6, p. 109).

The Teacher Training Agency (TTA)   The national body set up in 1994 to plan, fund and supervise teacher education and to commission research on teaching (see Chapter 4, p. 65).

Registered Inspector   An inspector who has qualified to lead a school inspection (not necessarily an HMI) (see Chapter 6, p. 119).

The General Teaching Council (GTC)   A body supported by most teacher associations which it is believed, could regulate all professional matters but which, as yet, lacks the endorsement of central government.

Local educational roles and structures

Local Education Authority (LEA)   The planning authority for education within a local government area which provides many 'central services' to teachers, schools, governors, parents and pupils (see Chapter 6, p. 107).

Education committee   The committee of elected councillors within a local government area which sets local education policy or interprets national policy for implementation by the LEA.

Chief Education Officer (CEO)/Director of Education   The chief executive of a Local Education Authority.

LEA Advisers   LEA educationalists providing professional support to teachers and governors for 'school improvement'.

LEA Inspectors   LEA educationalists who inspect school performance and report locally.

Education Officers   LEA administrators who administer and advise schools on organizational systems relating, for instance, to pupil admissions, staff appointments, school budgets and central provision for children with special educational needs.

Education Welfare Officers (EWO)   LEA staff with particular responsibilities for pupil attendance and general welfare through close liaison with Social Services, schools and families.

Social Services   A department within a local government area which is responsible for, among many other things, children's welfare (in the home) under the terms of the Children Act 1989.

Higher Education Institutions (HEIs)   Colleges and universities offering degrees, many of which also provide courses for initial teacher training in partnership with schools and courses to support the continuing professional development of teachers.

School types

Nursery school   A school offering suitable, but non-statutory, educational provision for children aged 2 to 4, including play, activity and language development. The recommended child–adult ratio is 13:1.

Nursery unit   A unit, offering suitable educational provision for children aged 3 and 4, which is attached to a school for older children.

Infant school   A school for children aged 5 to 7 in which Key Stage 1 of the National Curriculum is taught and assessed.

Junior school   A school for children aged 7 to 11 in which Key Stage 2 of the National Curriculum is taught and assessed.

Primary school   A school for children aged 5 to 11 in which Key Stage 1 and Key Stage 2 of the National Curriculum are taught and assessed.

First school   A school for children aged 5 to 8, or 5 to 9 in which appropriate parts of the Key Stage 1 and Key Stage 2 National Curriculum are taught and assessed.

Middle school   A school for children aged 8 to 12 or 9 to 13 in which appropriate parts of the Key Stage 2 and Key Stage 3 National Curriculum are taught and assessed.

Special school   A school for children of any age who have 'statements' of special educational needs. The National Curriculum may be taught, parts of it 'disapplied' to particular children or they may be 'exempted'.

Preparatory school   An independent school often catering for children from 5 to 13 years old in preparation for secondary education in 'public schools' (also independent).

School status

Voluntary aided (VA)   A school owned by a voluntary organization, usually a church but largely financed by an LEA. The governing body employ the staff, control admissions and determine the form of religious education (see Chapter 6, p. 109).

Voluntary controlled (VC)   A school set up by a voluntary organization, often the Church of England, but totally funded by an LEA. The LEA employs the staff (see Chapter 6, p. 109).

County   A school set up, owned and funded by an LEA.

Maintained   A school for which an LEA has financial and administrative responsibility (see Chapter 6, p. 108).

Grant maintained   A school which has 'opted out' of its LEA and receives funding from a national body, the Funding Agency for Schools (see Chapter 6, p. 109).

Independent   A privately owned school funded by fees paid by parents, for which conformity to many requirements of the national education system is not obligatory.

School funding and its implications

The local government settlement   The finance which is made available annually by national government from general taxation to support local government expenditure. Education usually accounts for a high proportion of such funding.

Council Tax   The means by which local governments raise funds from their electorate to contribute to their expenditure on local services, such as education.

Aggregated schools budget   The total funds made available for expenditure by schools by an LEA. This must be at least 85 per cent of its overall funding for education and is allocated using an approved funding formula (see Chapter 6, p. 113).

Formula funding   The method by which funds for school budgets are calculated, with a particular emphasis on numbers of pupils on roll as reflected in age weighted pupil units (see Chapter 6, p. 113).

Age weighted pupil units (AWPUs)   The number of 'units' allocated to children of particular ages which is reflected in levels of school funding. In 1995 a 16-year-old counted for nine units and a 7-year-old for one unit (see Chapter 6, p. 114).

Teacher salaries   A School Teachers' Review Body makes recommendation to the Secretary of State for Education each year on teachers' pay. In 1995 the range across the 'pay spine' for qualified teachers was from £11,883 to £32,169 in 17 points. Headteacher and deputy headteacher salaries are fixed and are in relation to the size of the school.

Pupil-teacher ratios   The proportion of pupils to *all* teachers in a school or within an education system – a figure which includes teachers in administrative or other posts.

Class size   The number of children in a class who are taught by one teacher. Often aggregated for a school, LEA or the national system to produce an average figure. The national figure for England has been rising in recent years (see Chapter 5, p. 95).

School management

Governing body   The group of parents, LEA, community representatives and teachers set up under the terms of School's Articles of Government to direct school policy and oversee school management (see Education Act 1986 and Chapter 6, p. 106).

Headteachers   The senior teacher and leader of school staff who is responsible for the implementation of National Curriculum and assessment requirements, school policies as set by governors, school staff, external liaison and effective use of financial and other resources (see Chapter 6, p. 110).

Deputy headteacher   A teacher who has been specifically appointed to deputize for the headteacher and who is likely to have been delegated a range of important management functions by the headteacher, as well as normally maintaining responsibility for a class of children.

Senior management teams (SMT)   A small group of senior staff in a school, normally receiving additional pay allowances, who support the headteacher in implementing school policies by acting as 'middle managers' (see Chapter 6, p. 110).

School ethos   The taken-for-granted pattern of values, inter-personal relationships and expectations about the education being provided which gives each school a particular subjective 'feel'. Often very influenced by the headteacher (see Chapter 2, p. 22).

School development plans (SDPs) An annual form of whole-school evaluation and planning, promoted by government and LEAs and expected to be produced by the headteacher, teachers and governors together (see Chapter 6, p. 114).

School policies Guidelines for action and practice within a school. Some policies are legally required and must be set by governors (see Chapter 6, p. 108).

Action plan A plan, prepared by a school's governors, following an OFSTED inspection to address any issues raised (see Chapter 6, p. 120).

Open enrolment A national requirement that all maintained schools must admit children whose parents wish it, until their standard number is reached (see Chapter 5, p. 93).

Admission The process of admitting children into the roll of the school, which must be carried out by each school in accordance with LEA policies. Parents are able to appeal if their child is refused a place at the school of their choice.

Exclusion The process of banning a pupil from a school. This may be either temporary or permanent and is usually initiated by the headteacher, often on disciplinary grounds.

Transfer The process of movement from one school to another.

Accountability Various processes by which teachers, schools or governors are required to justify their practices, policies and performance to others and in particular parents, including reports on pupil progress, convening of an annual meeting for parents and publishing OFSTED inspection reports (see Chapter 6).

Added value The measured gain in pupil attainment when performance on admission to a school is compared with performance at the point of transfer out. Seen as preferable to simple 'raw' attainment data because it allows for socio-economic and other contextual influences on pupil capability and thus indicates the school contribution (see Chapter 3, p. 58).

Standard number   The number of pupils which, based on the capacity of its buildings, a school is deemed to be able to accommodate.

School effectiveness   A judgement or measure of the efficiency of the school overall in producing educational outcomes given the characteristics of its pupil intake and the resources which are deployed. (see Chapter 3, p. 58).

People in primary schools

Parents

Parental rights   Legal rights under the 'Parents Charter' (1991) include the right to information about schools and pupil performance and the right to 'choose' a school to which to send their child (see Chapter 5, p. 58).

Parent-teacher partnership   A form of co-operative liaison, commonly promoted in primary schools, particularly to support the early stages of literacy but beneficial in enhancing all forms of pupil learning (see Chapter 5, p. 100).

Parent teacher associations (PTAs)   A voluntary organization normally set up to support a school with fund-raising activities and through encouraging parent-teacher co-operation (see Chapter 5, p. 98).

Community culture   The perceptions, values and social practices in a community which can affect a school considerably through the ways in which education is thought about and valued.

Governors

Instrument of government   The legal document which specifies the composition of governing bodies and defines the rules and procedures through which they function.

Chair of governors   A governor who is elected annually to chair meetings and represent the governing body between meetings.

Parent governor   A parent who has been elected by other parents of pupils at a school, to serve on the governing body (see Chapter 6, p. 107).

Local Education Authority governor   A school governor who has been appointed, and can be removed, by the LEA. Normally these appointments reflect the balance of political representation in the area.

Minor authority governor   A school governor who is a representative of a minor authority, such as a parish council.

Teacher governor   A governor who is a teacher at the school and has been elected by his or her colleagues.

Headteacher governor   A headteacher has a right to attend all meetings of the governing body and is a governor unless he or she opts not to be.

Co-opted governor   A governor of a county or controlled school who is added to the governing body by other governors for a particular reason, such as having relevant expertise, representing an underrepresented part of the community, etc.

Foundation governor   A governor who has been appointed, and can be removed, by the church or other organization which provides the school.

Clerk of governors The secretary to the governing body who issues agendas and compiles minutes.

Quorum The minimum number of governors who must be present for most decisions to be taken as a governing body – usually a third of all governors, rounded up.

Governors' subcommittees Groups of governors who meet between meetings of the full governing body to work on particular aspects of a schools affairs, such as staffing, curriculum, finance, sites and buildings. They report back to the governing body.

Pupils

Child culture The perceptions, values and social practices of children, for instance, developing in the playground or community which can affect friendship and social adjustment to school (see Chapter 2, p. 28).

Child perspectives on curriculum Young primary-aged children like to express themselves through play, artistic media and activity (see Chapter 3, p. 47).

Child perspectives on teachers Children often think of whether teachers are 'strict' or 'soft', whether they are 'fair' and whether they are 'kind'. Children also watch carefully for teacher mood so that they can predict what the teacher might do next (see Chapter 2, p. 29).

Child perspectives on assessment Children who are confident often welcome assessment, particularly if a teacher offers praise. Children who feel more vulnerable tend to feel uneasy about it, particularly in public situations.

Teachers

Initial teacher training (ITT)   The basic training to become a teacher. The established routes are via a BEd of three or four years or via a PGCE of one year following a degree. Courses are run in 'partnership' with schools and have large school-based elements (see Chapter 4, p. 65).

Qualified teacher status (QTS)   The professional qualification awarded following a course of teacher training which has been recognized by the Teacher Training Agency.

Induction period   The early years of a newly qualified teacher's professional work during which time particular training and support may be available, perhaps through a mentor.

Teachers' conditions of service   Contractual requirements made of teachers, set by the Secretary of State on the advice of the School Teachers' Review Body.

Teacher associations   The trade unions which represent teachers' interests as employees; the National Union of Teachers has the largest membership in primary schools.

Teacher culture   The perception, values and social practices of teachers, for instance developing in the staffroom, which can affect work commitment, classroom practice and school ethos.

Teacher appraisal   The process of assessing how a teacher is performing and attempting to match personal and institutional needs for future development.

In-service education for teachers (INSET)   The training and professional development activities of teachers working in schools, often in the form of short courses on in-school activities (see Chapter 4, p. 66).

Continuing professional development (CPD)   On-going, provision of progressive activities to ensure appropriate staff development throughout a teacher's career.

Supply teachers   Qualified teachers who are not in full-time teaching posts who make themselves available for occasional work to cover for absent school staff.

Other school staff

Nursery nurses   Specialists who have qualified in the education and development of pre-school aged children (NNEB), and who sometimes work in primary schools under the direction of a teacher.

Non-teaching assistants (NTA)   Staff who support teachers in their classroom work but who do not have formal teaching qualifications.

Special teaching assistants (STA)   Non-teaching assistants who work with particular children who have been identified as having special educational needs.

School secretaries   Staff who support the work of the head-teacher and deal with many facets of routine school administration, from greeting parents, simple first aid, typing letters and maintaining budget records.

School caretakers   Staff who have responsibility for daily maintenance and security of a school.

School cleaners   Cleaners, normally employed by a company who have won a contract to clean a school.

School meals supervisory assistants (SMSAs)   Staff employed to supervise children at dinner times.

Classroom issues for teaching and learning Curriculum

Curriculum concepts

Breadth Breadth exists when a curriculum provides pupils with teaching and learning experiences across a full range of subjects and activities. It is not narrow, such as focused on basic, or core, subjects only (see Chapter 3, p. 40).

Balance Balance exists when a curriculum provides pupils with appropriate proportions of teaching and learning across a full range of subjects and activities (see Chapter 3, p. 40).

Relevance Relevance exists when a curriculum is seen by pupils to meet their present and/or future needs (see Chapter 3, p. 37).

Coherence Coherence exists when the taught elements of a curriculum relate together in a logical and meaningful way (see Chapter 3, p. 37).

Integration Integration exists when a curriculum is constructed from the exploration of overlaps and juxtaposition of discrete subjects (see Chapter 3, p. 35).

Differentiation Differentiation is the provision of a range of curricular tasks or activities which are matched appropriately with the previous attainments of pupils (see Chapter 4, p. 70).

Progression Progression is a quality of a curriculum which extends children's knowledge, skills or understanding through an ordered sequential process (see Chapter 3, p. 40).

Continuity Continuity is the linkage which should exist when new subject matter or experiences are introduced into a programme of teaching and learning. This is particularly difficult when children move between classes or schools (see Chapter 3, p. 45).

Knowledge Knowledge, in curricular terms, is a selection of factual information which it is deemed to be appropriate for children to learn. In the National Curriculum this is reflected in its 'subjects' (see Chapter 3, p. 35).

Concepts Generalizations used to categorize things and events in order to think about them more effectively (see Chapter 3, p. 35).

Skills Skills are capacities to perform tasks, such as the 'motor skill' of forming letters correctly when handwriting, the 'oral skill' of a clear spoken explanation or the 'analytical skills' used in assessing historical evidence (see Chapter 3, p. 35).

Understanding Understanding is the sense which children are able to construct following experience or instruction (see Chapter 1).

Attitudes Attitudes are overt expressions of values and other personal qualities which tend to be adopted in a variety of situations. Children's attitudes to learning, for instance, can be vital (see Chapter 3, p. 35).

Curriculum processes

Curriculum audit A type of stock-taking procedure in which a school documents and reflectively analyses its whole curriculum provision (see Chapter 6, p. 115).

Curriculum development A development process, often focused on a particular subject area, on which a staff team work to improve curriculum provision.

Whole-school curriculum planning A holistic planning process involving all teaching staff to ensure breadth, balance, coherence, relevance, differentiation and progression in an area of curriculum.

Planning classroom schemes of work The production of a detailed classroom plan for curricular work by a teacher for a particular unit of time.

Forms of curriculum

The whole curriculum A conception of the overall curriculum with particular concern for its coherence and for the inter-relationship of subjects.

Subject study Classroom work which focuses on discrete subject content, perhaps to maximize progression in teaching and learning (see Chapter 4, p. 71).

Project work Classroom work which reaches across subjects in an attempt to maximize the relevance and coherence of teaching and learning activities (see Chapter 3, p. 35).

Extra-curricular activities Activities which take place, often run by teachers, outside the time which is officially allocated for classroom work.

Hidden curriculum A conception of all the things that are learned at school *beyond* the overt curriculum of subjects, for instance about values, interpersonal relationships and behaviour in the classroom and in the school as a whole, and in respect of issues such as gender, social class, ethnicity and ability (see Chapter 2, p. 25).

The National Curriculum The knowledge, skills, concepts and attitudes, which are laid down by statutory orders following the Education Reform Act 1988, that children in maintained schools should be taught (see Chapter 3, p. 40).

The National Curriculum framework

Statutory orders   A form of legislative requirement of schools, set by the Secretary of State for Education and requiring the approval of Parliament. They have the same legal force as an Act of Parliament.

Core foundation subjects   English, maths and science (see Chapter 3, p. 43, and Chapter 9).

Other foundation subjects   Technology, history, geography, music, art, physical education and, in Wales, Welsh (see Chapter 3, p. 43, and Chapter 9).

Programmes of study (PoS)   Everything which the National Curriculum requires must be taught to pupils during each Key Stage for them to satisfy the attainment targets for each subject (see Chapter 9).

Modification and disapplication   Terms used to lift part or all of the National Curriculum requirements for individuals or schools as approved by the Secretary of State for Education.

Attainment targets (ATs)   Objectives for each subject which set out the knowledge, skills and understanding which pupils are expected to develop with that area of the National Curriculum (see Chapter 3, p. 46).

Levels (of attainment)   The expected range of attainment at the end of Key Stage 1 is from Levels 1 to 3, at the end of Key Stage 2 from Levels 2 to 5 and at the end of Key Stage 3 from 3 to 7. Level 8 provides for very able pupils at Key Stage 3. These are the stepped sequence of eight levels used in assessment procedures covering children's expected development from Key Stage 1 to Key Stage 3 of all National Curriculum subjects with the exception of art, music and physical education. The latter are covered by end of Key Stage descriptions only and assessment by level is not required (see Chapter 3, p. 49).

Level descriptions (LDs)   Descriptions of the knowledge, skill and understanding which is expected to be characteristic of eight levels of attainment for each National Curriculum attainment target. Used for assessment procedures in which teachers judge the 'best fit' of level descriptors with known pupil attainments (see Chapter 3, p. 51).

End of Key Stage descriptions (EKSDs)   Statements, for some subjects only, of the knowledge, skill and understanding which it is expected children will acquire by the end of each Key Stage.

Key Stage   The periods in each pupil's education to which the National Curriculum applies. For primary aged pupils Key Stage 1 is from the start of school to age 7 (Reception, Year 1, Year 2) and Key Stage 2 is from age 7 to age 11 (Year 3, Year 4, Year 5, Year 6).

Religious education   In each LEA, a multi-faith Standing Advisory Council on Religious Education (SACRE) advises on religious education and collective worship and produces an 'agreed syllabus' for the use of schools. This must be 'in the main Christian' whilst taking account of other 'principal religions' in the UK.

Other curriculum content issues

Basic skills   A term usually taken to denote the '3Rs' (reading, 'riting and 'rithmetic) of the old elementary school tradition.

Cross-curricular issues   Issues and concerns which are of great importance and about which teaching and learning may occur in many different subjects.

Personal and social education (PSE)   A cross-curricular issue concerning the holistic development of the child beyond the curriculum and with particular reference to self-perception and interrelationships with others.

Sex education Curricular provision, reflecting the school policy set by governors, which introduces children to sex and human relationships and encourages them to consider morals and the value of family life.

Multicultural education An approach to teaching and curriculum provision intended to increase all pupil's awareness and appreciation of the cultures, beliefs and traditions of the ethnic groups in British society. Sometimes criticized for failing to address the 'real' structural issues of social disadvantage that many minority British ethnic groups face.

Anti-racist education An approach to teaching and curriculum provision intended to increase all pupil's awareness and understanding of the socio-economic structures which systematically and institutionally disadvantage many minority British ethnic groups. Sometimes criticized for being too radical.

Education for citizenship A National Curriculum theme intended to establish the importance of 'positive, participative citizenship' through work on topics such as: community, democracy in action, the law, living in a plural society, work and employment.

Environmental education A National Curriculum theme intended to promote 'positive and responsible attitudes towards the environment'. It aims to increase knowledge and understanding of processes of environmental change.

Economic and industrial understanding A National Curriculum theme intended to 'prepare pupils for their future roles as producers, consumers and citizens in a democracy'. Work in primary schools often begins with encouraging children to organize their own finances or learn about the 'world of work'.

Health education   A National Curriculum theme intended to 'inculcate the values of a healthy mind in a healthy body'. This includes work on sex education, drug, family life, safety, health-related exercise, nutrition and personal hygiene.

Pedagogy

General approaches to teaching

Fitness for purpose   The approach advocated in a 1992 report, *Curriculum Organisation and Classroom Practice in Primary Schools*, by Alexander, Rose and Woodhead, which steps aside from the polarized debates about approaches to teaching which have beset primary education. It argues that all approaches have strengths and weaknesses and that teachers should adopt whatever is likely to be most suitable for their particular educational purpose. There are no easy, 'right' answers (see Chapter 4, p. 72).

Progressive teaching   This is a very general term which is usually associated with allowing considerable amounts of child activity and choice with the teacher in the role of facilitator. Associated with 'child-centred education' and 'discovery methods' it was thought to have been prevalent in primary school classrooms following the Plowden Report of 1967. However, HMI inspections and research studies found little evidence, though it was, and is, important in teachers' professional commitment to pupils and the quality of their experiences in school.

Traditional teaching   A very general term which is usually associated with rather didactic methods in which a teacher controls the curriculum and pupil behaviour very tightly and adopts the role of instructor. Associated with the preparatory and elementary traditions in primary education and sometimes believed to be associated with 'higher standards', though, even if others allowed this, they would add 'and a narrow curriculum'.

Child-centred education Another general term, associated with progressive teaching, and used to denote provision which is designed around sets of assumptions about the needs of the children of a particular age. The approach was influenced by Piaget's thinking and has been very influential in shaping teacher's values and commitments to children (see Chapter 4, p. 63).

Didactic teaching A form of teaching with tight teacher control in which knowledge is transmitted to the pupil, who is expected to passively receive it and to 'read, mark, learn and inwardly digest' the knowledge. Closely associated with traditional teaching (see Chapter 1, p. 9; Chapter 4, p. 72).

Forms of school organization of classes

Single age classes A class of pupils, often formed in a school with one form of entry at admission, in which all the pupils have birthdays in the same school year.

Mixed age classes A class of pupils, common in schools which do not have one complete form of entry at admission, in which the pupils have birthdays in more than one school year. Mixed age classes are very common in primary schools, particularly in small, rural schools.

Streaming An organizational device in which a judgement of 'general ability' is used to allocate the children in a school or year-group to broad groups for *all* teaching purposes. This approach was popular in the 1950s and early 1960s in preparation of some children for 11+ exams, though less able children often suffered from reduced self-esteem.

Mixed ability classes Classes formed by a mixture of pupils attending a school, with no attempt at differentiation on the basis of attainment or ability. The most common form of class organization in primary schools and valued for the sense of community and understanding of others which it can engender.

Setting A process whereby children are taught a particular subject in groups, based on their attainment or on a judgement of ability. Once an important feature of traditional teaching and its suitability for some purposes is now being reconsidered.

Targeting A recently developed process, elaborated from setting, whereby children are taught in particular groups for very specific purposes. Having been 'targeted', they then return to mixed ability classes for other activities.

Teaching roles

Generalist class teacher A teacher who teaches *all* subjects of the National Curriculum to his or her class of children. Allows great flexibility and is often associated with the statement that 'I teach children not subjects'. Reflects the assertion of an important quality in the commitment of primary school teachers to the social and emotional development of children. Particularly common in work with young children, where the balance of advantage is seen to lie with generalism and knowing the personalities of the children very well.

Specialist subject teacher A teacher who specializes in the teaching of a limited number of National Curriculum subjects and teaches them to several classes across the school. Part of a small team of specialist subject teachers so that the whole curriculum is covered by careful timetabling. Strong in the preparatory tradition and becoming more common since the introduction of the National Curriculum, particularly in work with older children, where the balance of advantage is seen to lie with specialism and knowing the subject to be studied very well.

Semi-specialist teacher A hybrid of generalist and specialist in which the roles are enacted selectively for particular purposes. For instance, four teachers in a junior school may teach English, maths and some topics which integrate history, geography, technology and art as a generalist to their own class. However, music, science, physical education and information technology may be taught by these same four teachers, working in each other's classrooms so that each can share a particular expertise which he or she has.

Forms of class organization of pupils

Whole-class work   A form of organization in which a whole class is taught together or works on similar tasks or activities together.

Group work   A form of class organization in which individual pupils work in a group on tasks or activities which are similar.

Co-operative group work   A form of class organization in which individual pupils work in a group and contribute to a shared task or activity which has been set for the group as a whole.

Individualized work   A form of class organization in which each individual pupil is set particular tasks or activities.

Elements of lessons

Orientation   An early point of a lesson in which children are prepared for the topic they are to be taught.

Instruction   An important, structuring or restructuring element of a lesson in which the teacher clarifies aims, offers the pupils knowledge, skill and understanding of the subject and sets aims for tasks and/or activities. A phase which may be revisited if particular teacher support during a lesson is required (see Chapter 4, p. 70).

Tasks   A clearly defined structure for learning which has been set up by a teacher and which has a specified objective which is known to the pupil. More common with older children (see Chapter 4, p. 71).

Activities   A relatively open-ended structure for learning, often involving use of a resource or medium which has been provided by the teacher for general experiential purposes and within which children can often introduce their own objectives. More common with younger children.

Review An opportunity to consider the processes and outcomes which have resulted from engagement in tasks and activities. In particular, pupils can articulate and hear about developments in knowledge, understanding and skill, thus leading to consolidation. The teachers can gather evidence to help them assess pupil progress which can be used in future lessons.

Teaching strategies

Instructing Imparting knowledge, skill or understanding to enhance the development of a learner.

Observing Watching a learner carefully to inform a judgement of their responses to a learning challenge.

Explaining Providing clarification in response to a learner's need.

Discussing Engaging with learners in focused conversation on a learning topic with a view to enhancing their knowledge, skill, understanding or motivation.

Questioning Asking a learner questions to diagnose his or her existing level of knowledge, skill or understanding, or to gauge his or her attitude and motivation towards a learning challenge.

Conferencing Holding a particular conversation with an individual pupil for the purpose of reviewing his or her learning progress and to plan future targets.

Scaffolding Providing appropriate support, often though instruction or explanation, which enables a child to construct understanding for themselves. Often thought of in association with Vygotsky's concept of the 'zone of proximal development' (see Chapter 1, p. 13).

Matching   Ensuring that learning tasks are set at suitable levels of challenge in respect of pupils' existing knowledge, skills and understanding.

Reflecting   Taking stock of teaching and learning, evaluating evidence and analysing strengths and weaknesses in classroom provision and teaching practices.

Psychological approaches to learning

Behaviourism   A psychological approach based on study of how animals respond to environmental stimuli and can become 'conditioned'. Early investigators were Watson, Pavlov and Skinner. Sophisticated chains of such learning are possible, particularly in people, and behaviourism has been a dominant form of psychology since the early 1900s (see Chapter 1, p. 10).

Constructivism   A psychological approach based on the study of children's attempts to construct understanding through inter-action with their environment of people, things and experiences. The most influential constructivist was Piaget who, among other things, studied the role of language on children's thinking and who generated a model of four 'stages' in children's intellectual development (see Chapter 2, p. 11: Chapter 4, p. 73).

Social constructivism   A psychological approach which locates many constructivist ideas within a social context to emphasize the influence of culture and interaction on learning. The most influential social constructivist was Vygotsky who, in particular, conceived of the 'zone of proximal development' (ZPD) and emphasized the role of a more knowledgeable other (teacher, parent or child) in scaffolding a learner's understanding (see Chapter 2, p. 11; Chapter 4, p. 75).

Child development   A general psychological approach which traces the interaction of physical, intellectual, social and emotional development of children. Once particularly central to initial teacher education for what may seem to be obvious reasons, it has been largely excluded from courses in recent years as a result of government regulation and the wish to emphasize the teaching of subjects.

Psychological issues and concepts

Intelligence   The capability to know, do and understand. Once thought of as being a general capability largely deriving from genetic inheritance, modern thinking suggests the existence of multiple forms of intelligence and of significant social influences on their development.

Language   The verbal expression of thought and feeling for communication. A medium which plays a central role in the development of cognition and social interaction from birth (see Chapter 1).

Experience   Engagement with people, materials, events and the environment which is formative in shaping the perception and responses of learners (see Chapter 1, p. 10).

Motivation   The disposition of learners to learn, often variable in respect of particular topics.

Schema   A framework of existing thinking and interconnected concepts held by a learner, into which successive learning may be assimilated.

Meta-cognition   The process by which an individual reflects on the process of his or her thinking, which can have a powerful effect in improving the quality of that thinking.

The zone of proximal development (ZPD)   The area which is just beyond a learner's existing level of knowledge, skill or understanding and which they could successfully learn about if appropriately supported by a knowledgeable other (see Chapter 1, p. 11).

Self-esteem   The value or opinion which an individual ascribes to himself or herself, thus powerfully influencing self-confidence in tackling new learning challenges (see Chapter 1, p. 17).

Creativity   The element of originality, innovation or divergence which a learner is able to apply to a learning challenge.

Cognition   The psycho-biological process of thinking and processing information which is involved in all learning by individuals.

Affects   Feelings held by individuals, for instance, in the experience of learning and social interaction.

Play   An activity, particularly common among young children, in which ideas, roles, behaviour and the imagination can be explored with minimal risk (see Chapter 2, p. 10).

Discipline   A constraint on behaviour, imposed by self or others, which is essential in a school environment because it enables teachers and pupils to concentrate on learning (see Chapter 4, p. 68).

Assessment

Assessment concepts

Attainment   The level of achievement reached by a child in respect of a sequence of learning.

Achievement   The progress which a child has made in meeting learning challenges.

Ability   The capacity which a child has to learn, which may be specific to particular areas of learning.

Forms of assessment

Entry assessment   Assessment procedures used when children enter school aged 4 or 5 for diagnostic purposes and to provide a baseline for later calculation of progress made and 'added value' (see Chapter 3, p. 58).

Formative assessment   Continuous assessment, often in diverse, non-standardized forms, made for the purpose of informing ongoing teaching (see Chapter 3, p. 49).

Summative assessment   Assessment procedures, often at the end of a programme of teaching and of a consistent or standardized type, used to assess learning outcomes (see Chapter 3, p. 49).

Self-assessment   Assessment by a learner for the purpose of self-knowledge, reflection and self-improvement.

Teacher assessment (TA)   A form of formative assessment required of teachers by the Education Reform Act the results of which are reported to parents and have parity with SAT results (see below and Chapter 3, p. 50).

Standardized assessment tests and tasks (SATs)   A form of summative assessment used to test pupil learning of the core subjects of the National Curriculum at the end of Key Stages. The results are reported to parents and have parity with TA results (see above and Chapter 3, p. 53).

Forms of recording

Portfolio of work   A folder or collection of documents, records or artefacts relating to a pupil's work over several years. Items collected are often carefully selected after consultation with the child and annotated. Often used formatively in discussions between parents, teachers and child and for self-assessment (see Chapter 3, p. 59).

Records of achievement (RoA)   A semi-public record of achievements and attainments by a child over a course of time, perhaps in a school. Sometimes used to affirm and celebrate and often with a more summative, certificated feel than a portfolio.

Teacher records   A teacher-controlled record system devised to assist in planning, providing and monitoring an appropriate curriculum for each pupil.

Forms of reporting

Parents' evenings   Very common practice where parents get the opportunity to talk briefly to their child's teacher about their progress and discuss any difficulties (see Chapter 5).

Written reports   An annual document from school to parents summarizing the achievements and attainment of each pupil (see Chapter 5).

League tables of pupil attainment   Tables, often published in newspapers, in which schools are ranked in order of their aggregate levels of pupil attainment at a public assessment point, such as at the end of Key Stage 2. This is relatively simple to do, but tends to reflect the social circumstances of the pupil intake more than the particular contribution of the schools (see Chapter 3, p. 57).

League tables of added value   Tables, sometimes published in newspapers, in which schools are ranked in terms of levels of pupil attainment at the end of a programme of study compared with their levels of attainment at the beginning of the programme of study. This reveals the gain, or added value but is technically difficult to produce (see Chapter 3, p. 58).

League tables of rolling averages   A proposed form of table, in which a rolling average of, say, three years of aggregated data on pupil attainment would be published, thus providing some stabilization in variability and showing trends in attainment results from the pupils of each school.

Social issues, concepts, processes and consequences

Equality of opportunity

The principle that all people, irrespective for instance of ethnicity, gender, disability or social class, should have equal access to opportunities – including educational opportunities. Equality of opportunity is an ideal and a commitment, but it has been undermined by the spread of poverty and by some education policies in England and Wales in recent years (see Chapter 7, p. 129).

Entitlement

The principle that all citizens have a right to certain forms of provision, for instance, of parents and pupils to good schools and high-quality teaching, and of teachers to adequate resources and sound education policies (see Chapter 3, p. 40).

Fulfilment of potential

The aspiration that all individuals will be able to fulfil themselves and develop in all the ways which they can during their lives. This aspiration is compromised if opportunities are unequal or if entitlements are not protected.

Underachievement

The extent to which potential is unfulfilled, and a significant problem in the UK. However, it is a complex problem and, among other things, requires attention to structural issues concerning the culture, values and socio-economic conditions in some communities and to the resources available to some schools.

Low expectations

An explanation for underachievement which is often offered by governments and which primarily locates the problem with teachers and parents, but less with governments.

Vocational development

Educational provision which is specifically designed to support pupils in future work and employment.

Social development

Educational provision which is specifically designed to support the social adjustment and self-confidence of pupils (see Chapter 1, p. 14).

Special educational needs (SEN)

Particular physical, emotional or intellectual needs which a child has been assessed as having. Children for whom a 'statement' of needs has been issued are entitled to have their needs met by their LEA subject to the 'efficient use of resources' (see Chapter 2, p. 31).

Interests

The concerns and priorities which individuals or groups may have in defence or promotion of a structural position which they occupy in society. This may be a useful concept in analysing contributions to educational controversies and debates.

Power

The capacity which an individual or group has to get or make others do what they wish. Often, as in education, there are 'power struggles' in which many people and groups have some power and outcomes are resolved by a process of shifting alliances as events unfold. However, since the Education Reform Act the Secretary of State for Education has had an unprecedented number of powers.

Ideology

A set of ideas and beliefs which is often held by social groups who share particular interests. Seen therefore as a source of bias and irrationality. In respect of primary education, the late 1980s and early 1990s saw a constant stream of accusations of ideological bias by government ministers of teachers and by teachers of government ministers. They were probably both right to some extent (see Chapter 3, on the curriculum and assessment struggles, and Chapter 4 regarding teaching methods).

Social status

The ascribed esteem in which an individual or social position is held. This can be important to children in their peer group (see Chapter 2, p. 29) and it is important to teachers in society more generally (see Chapter 4, p. 62).

Socialization

The process by which individuals are inducted into the taken-for-granted rules, values and cultural understandings of a group or social organization. This is particularly relevant to teachers and pupils entering schools and taking on new roles. However, such individuals should not be seen as being entirely passive (see Chapter 2, p. 24).

Perspectives

The cluster of subjective opinions and meanings with which an individual or group make sense of an experience, of something or of somebody. This is important for all those involved in a school, and, in particular for the partnership of parents, pupils and teachers in learning.

Social differentiation

A generic term for the process, in education, by which teachers identify and separate groups of pupils for particular purposes. For instance, to study particular subjects for matching ability levels or for control purposes. In the long term, this can affect opportunities and life-chances.

Polarization

A generic term for the process in education by which children, operating through peer culture, tend to reinforce social differentiation and amplify its consequences through their friendships and social relationships.

Teacher expectations

The beliefs which a teacher holds about the possible performance of his or her pupils. Pupil attainment is thought to be influenced by these.

Coping strategies

The patterned ways in which teachers and pupils act in classrooms and schools to protect their personal interests and perspectives.

Social class

A concept used to denote the types and range of social, cultural and economic resource and the distribution of political power among social groups in societies. This is of relevance to education in the UK in the 1990s because inequalities have been growing and educational underachievement is adversely affecting working-class children, particularly in inner cities (see Chapter 2, p. 30).

Gender

A concept used to denote the social expectations which are associated with males and females in a society. This is of relevance to primary education in the UK for many reasons. For instance, women teachers, though more numerous, seem to be disadvantaged in reaching senior positions in schools. However, girls are now outperforming boys in school attainment in many subjects, raising different sorts of gender issues (see Chapter 2, p. 30).

Ethnicity

A concept used to denote the cultural and racial reference group or groups with which an individual is identified, but which in law, has nothing to do with citizenship. This is of relevance to education in the UK because there is evidence of variation in the attainment of pupils from different ethnic groups (see Chapter 2, p. 30).

Disability

A concept used to highlight the needs of people who may be physically or mentally disabled and for whom access to their educational entitlements may be restricted, despite possible statements of special educational need. This is of importance to education because of the responsibilities which remain to support disabled people in fulfilling their full potential.

Chapter 9

THE NATIONAL CURRICULUM FOR PRIMARY SCHOOLS IN ENGLAND AND WALES: A SYNOPSIS

There are many similarities in the national curricula of England and Wales, but they are not identical. For instance, the Welsh Cymreig was implemented with more consideration for the integration of subjects across the curriculum and with particular awareness of linguistic and cultural diversity. The English subject descriptions for English, maths, science, technology, information technology and physical education also apply in Wales. The Welsh versions of the National Curriculum for history, geography, art and music vary a little from the English versions. Welsh applies only in Wales, where it is a core subject.

For an overview and explanation of the structure of the National Curriculum, see Chapter 3, pp. 40–80.

The National Curriculum content: Core foundation subjects

English

Probably the most important subject in the primary school curriculum, on which research has often recorded over a third of classroom time is spent, particularly with the youngest children. It embraces the 'basic skills' of reading, writing, speaking and listening. Valued by parents, industry and teachers, English is the most carefully assessed subject in national procedures, and school and national performance results frequently arouse much public interest. This is a 'high stakes' subject. For this very reason, it can tend to dominate curricular provision and this is considered by some to threaten the intention that the National Curriculum should be 'broad and balanced'. On the other hand, English can be taught with and through all other subjects.

The National Curriculum sets out a programme of study for each of three attainment targets: 'speaking and listening', 'reading' and 'writing'. An indication of the content of each is given below and it is important to know that these programmes of study have been the subject of much political and professional debate, reflecting very disparate views of the role of language in education and society. The place of standard English, bilingualism and cultural diversity is particularly important and is also considered below.

Standard English

A contentious issue in the development of the National Curriculum in which positions were taken up between those who argued that standard English was necessary in the modern world and part of the national heritage and others who wanted the National Curriculum to affirm the value of the diverse cultures and languages which exist in modern Britain.

Regarding speaking and listening at Key Stage 1, the major settlement was the statement that 'pupils should be introduced *with appropriate sensitivity* to the importance of standard English' (my emphasis).

At Key Stage 2 pupils are required to be taught 'to be fluent, accurate users of standard English vocabulary and grammar, and to recognize its importance as the language of public communication' and 'should be taught to adapt their talk to suit different circumstances'.

Bilingualism and cultural diversity

Many people feel that the National Curriculum for English does not fully reflect and build upon the knowledge, skills and understandings which exist among the diverse cultural and ethnic groups living in the different regions and communities of England and Wales.

The 'general requirements' for the English National Curriculum assert a pupil entitlement to 'a full range of opportunities necessary to enable them to develop competence in standard English' and some have argued that knowledge of standard English helps to build national cohesion.

The National Curriculum requirement recognizes dialects and other languages but places them in a rather subservient position: 'The richness of dialects and other languages can make an important contribution to pupil's knowledge and understanding of standard English.'

Speaking and listening

As the first attainment target for English at Key Stage 1, talking and listening for a full range of purposes is encouraged in the programme of study, including the use of story, description, explanation and drama. Key skills of effective communication are addressed, including confident speaking and attentive listening.

At Key Stage 2 the range is developed to include debate and analysis used in a wider range of contexts, including those accessed through further drama. Key skills are now to be developed regarding responsiveness to audiences, in presentational skills and in terms of analysing the presentations of others.

For assessment purposes, there are level descriptions describing characteristic pupil attainments at speaking and listening.

Reading

As the second attainment target for English at Key Stage 1, children are to be 'given extensive experience of children's literature' with the support of adults, and should use books and computers to assemble information. The emphasis is on experience of a wide, rich experience of literature in many forms, such as poems and stories which are both traditional and from a range of different cultures. The key skills in learning to read which are identified are: contextual understanding, phonic knowledge, graphic knowledge, word recognition and grammatical knowledge.

At Key Stage 2 pupils are to be 'encouraged to develop as enthusiastic, independent and reflective readers' through extensive reading of more challenging fiction and non-fiction.

Their capacity to use the key skills should be extended and children should be encouraged to 'respond imaginatively to the plot, characters, ideas, vocabulary and organisation of language in literature' and to evaluate texts.

For assessment purposes, there are level descriptions describing characteristic pupil attainments at reading (see Figure 3.8, p. 52).

Writing

As the third attainment target for English at Key Stage 1, children are to be encouraged to see writing as 'a means of remembering, communicating, organising and developing ideas and information, and as a source of enjoyment'. They should be taught to write with 'confidence, fluency and accuracy' and should plan and review drafts of their writing. They should begin to learn about and develop knowledge and skills in punctuation, spelling and handwriting.

At Key Stage 2 writing for a range of purposes and audiences is emphasized. Key process skills in writing are to be taught: planning, drafting, revising, proof-reading and presenting a final copy. Punctuation, spelling and handwriting are to be further developed, for instance, in handwriting they should write with 'greater control and fluency' and 'use different forms of handwriting for different purposes'.

For assessment purposes, there are level descriptions describing characteristic pupil attainments at writing.

Welsh

Children in Welsh schools are to be taught to speak standard spoken Welsh and to develop an awareness of the literary heritage of Wales. An integrated programme of speaking, listening, viewing, reading and writing is to be developed.

At Key Stage 1, oral skills of speaking, listening and viewing should be developed and children should be taught how to speak clearly and made aware of language varieties around them. They should begin to learn to read, using context, the alphabet, knowledge of language, prediction, recall and discussion to create understanding. Pupils should use their writing to communicate experiences, opinions and information, constructing short, varied passages. They should discuss the content, expression, language and structure of their work and attempt to improve it. They should be taught to hold their pencil comfortably and begin to develop a legible style.

At Key Stage 2, the integrated programme is to be extended. Pupil awareness of language use in various media should be developed and they should develop awareness of the needs of different audiences. They should express and evaluate opinions, contribute to discussions and presentations. They should be taught to increase their awareness of variety in language. In reading, children should be taught to read a variety of books, prose and poetry confidently, meaningfully, fluently and with appropriate expression. They should develop their personal taste and responses to reading material and media. Pupils should be taught a variety of ways of writing including responding to media, artefacts, music and leisure, to write in personal and imaginative modes, to present information coherently and to express a point of view. In the context of their work they should write correctly and attend to grammar, style, punctuation and spelling. They should use the writing process of drafting, redrafting and editing after discussion.

For assessment purposes, there are level descriptions describing characteristic pupil attainments at Welsh.

Mathematics

This is another very important subject in the primary school curriculum which, as 'arithmetic', was a strong feature of provision in the old elementary tradition of the nineteenth century. Now considerably broadened in scope and enlivened in approaches to teaching and learning, it also has a growing significance in modern life. Pupils' work on maths has been found to take up about 15 per cent of classroom time at Key Stage 1, with this figure tending to rise at Key Stage 2.

At Key Stage 1 there are three attainment targets in the programme of study:

1. 'Using and applying mathematics' requires opportunities to be provided so that children can use maths in practical, problem-solving tasks and real-life situations as well as in maths itself. They should also be encouraged to talk about their work and to develop the ways in which they think about mathematics.
2. 'Number' requires pupils to be given opportunities to do such things as 'develop flexible methods of working with number, orally and mentally', use a calculator, record in a variety of ways and use computer software. They should be able to count and to read, write and order numbers, initially to ten but progressing up to 1,000. They should develop an understanding of place value, of the relationships between numbers and of ways of beginning computation. They should know simple addition and subtraction facts to 20 and begin to explore very simple multiplication and division. Pupils should be taught to solve simple numerical problems and to classify, represent and interpret data, such as through sorting into sets or constructing graphs.
3. 'Shape, space and measures' requires that pupils have access to a wide range of practical experiences and materials to develop their knowledge and understanding in these areas. They should understand and use patterns and shape, for instance, though learning the names and geometric features of simple shapes. They should be able to describe positions and recognize the implications of movement and turn through simple angles. They should be able to compare objects and events and begin to measure them using non-standard and standard units of length, mass and capacity.

At Key Stage 2 there are four attainment targets in the programme of study:

1. 'Using and applying mathematics' extends previous work to cover making and monitoring decisions to solve problems, developing mathematical language and forms of communication, and developing mathematical reasoning.
2. 'Number' extends pupils' early knowledge, skills and understanding, particularly of number structures. Teaching of

place value is to be developed and there is to be consideration of simple negative numbers, decimals and fractions. Understanding of the relationships between numbers is to be worked on and applied to various methods of computation. Multiplication facts are to be taught up to ten times ten. Mental methods of calculation with whole numbers up to 100 are to be developed and children should be able to solve numerical problems involving number, money or measures, by the use of addition, subtraction, multiplication and division, or a calculator where appropriate.

3. 'Shape, space and measures' extends children's understanding and capacity to use the properties of shape in 2-D and 3-D. They are to be taught more about the properties of position and movement, including rotation and the use of coordinates and angles. They must continue to develop their work on measures on length, mass, capacity and time and be able to make 'sensible estimates in everyday situations'.

4. 'Handling data' provides an introduction to representation, statistics, research and the use of computers. Pupils should be taught to collect, represent and interpret data in relation to issues of their choice arising in everyday life and to produce simple descriptive statistics about them. They should also begin to understand and calculate probability, through practical experience as well as through experiment and theory.

For assessment purposes, there are level descriptions describing characteristic pupil attainments for each area of the Mathematics programme of study.

Science

Science, as presented in the National Curriculum, is a relatively new subject in primary schools. Prior to the introduction of the National Curriculum it was taught in a very *ad hoc* manner, perhaps though nature study. Teachers' subject knowledge in this area has been weak but confidence has been developing though the 1990s. Studies have found that science work normally takes up a little under a tenth of pupils' learning time in primary school classrooms.

At Key Stage 1 there are four attainment targets in the programme of study:

1. 'Experimental and investigative science' requires that children should be taught to plan experimental work, obtain evidence and consider evidence.
2. 'Life processes and living things' requires attention to humans and green plants as organisms, to the variation and classification of living things and to the ways in which living things are influenced by their environment.
3. 'Materials and their properties' requires work on everyday uses of materials such as metal, plastic, wood, paper, glass, wool and rock. Understanding of different ways of grouping materials should be developed and the ways in which materials may change or be changed should be studied.
4. 'Physical processes' requires study of simple features of electricity, forces and motion and light and sound. For instance, children may make simple electric circuits, explore pushes and pulls though models, investigate sources of light and consider how to make and detect sounds.

At Key Stage 2 the same four attainment targets recur in the programme of study. However, enquiry is now encouraged to be more systematic and the idea of testing scientific ideas is to be developed:

1. 'Experimental and investigative science' extends the standard of inventiveness and precision which is expected of children when taught to plan experimental work, obtain evidence and consider evidence in scientific activity.
2. 'Life processes and living things' extends pupils' work on humans and green plants as organisms. Regarding humans, they are to be taught about nutrition, circulation, movement, growth and reproduction and health. Regarding green plants, they should learn about growth, nutrition and reproduction. Their work on variation and classification should be extended and, with regard to living things in their environ-

ment, they should be taught about adaption, feeding relationships and micro-organisms.

3. 'Materials and their properties' requires further study of the grouping and classifying of materials on a wider range of criteria and properties. Similarly, investigation of the conditions which bring about change in materials is required, and of the nature of the changes which are produced. Issues associated with the separation of mixtures of materials are to be introduced.

4. 'Physical processes' extend work on simple electrical circuits using switches, current regulation and representation. Treatment of forces and motion is extended to consider types of force and issues associated with balanced and unbalanced forces. Work on light is to be moved on to everyday effects of light and to seeing. On sound, pupils are to be taught about vibration. The Earth and beyond are to be taught with attention to the properties of the Sun, Earth and Moon and to periodic changes.

For assessment purposes, there are level descriptions describing characteristic pupil attainments for each attainment target in science.

The National Curriculum content: Other foundation subjects

History

This is a long-established subject in the primary curriculum, which has often been integrated with other subjects through topic work. The programme of study is broken down into two aspects, 'areas of study' which specify a focus on historical content, and 'key elements' which specify the development of historical skills. There is one attainment target for history within the programme of study; 'history'.

At Key Stage 1 the areas to be studied are very open; 'the everyday life, work, leisure and culture of men, women and children in the past'; different kinds of 'famous men and women, including personalities drawn from British history', and different types of past event. The key elements to be taught at a very simple level cover chronology, the range and depth of historical knowledge and understanding, interpretations and historical enquiry and ways of organizing and communicating historical understanding.

At Key Stage 2 the areas of study are specified in the form of study units. These are: Romans, Anglo-Saxons and Vikings in Britain; life in Tudor times; Victorian Britain or Britain since 1930; Ancient Greece; local history; and a past non-European society. Where appropriate, the history of Britain should be set in its European and world context and history should be viewed from a variety of perspectives. The key elements remain as in Key Stage 1 but are to be taught through the study units to more refined levels of skill, knowledge and understanding.

For assessment purposes, there are level descriptions describing characteristic pupil attainments for the attainment target in history.

In Wales pupils are to be given opportunities to develop and apply their knowledge and understanding of the cultural, economic, environmental and linguistic characteristics of Wales. Examples are to be drawn from Wales at Key Stage 1 and at Key Stage 2 there are study units about life in Wales.

Geography

This is a long-established subject in the primary curriculum, which has often been integrated with other subjects through topic work. The geography programmes of study for primary schools are divided into three elements: geographical skills, places and thematic study. There is only one attainment target in the programme of study: 'geography'.

At Key Stage 1 pupils should be taught to use geographical terms, undertake simple fieldwork, make maps and use some secondary sources. They should study the locality of the school and a contrasting locality from elsewhere in the UK or overseas. As a thematic study, they should investigate the quality of the environment in any locality.

At Key Stage 2 pupils should extend and practise their geographical skills and should study three localities: one normally including the area in which the pupils live; one contrasting elsewhere in the UK and one in Africa, Asia (excluding Japan),

South America or Central America (excluding the Caribbean). Thematic studies, which may be combined with the study of places or with other themes, should be of rivers, weather, settlement and environmental change.

For assessment purposes, there are level descriptions describing characteristic pupil attainments for the attainment target in geography.

In Wales pupils are to be given opportunities to develop and apply their knowledge and understanding of the cultural, economic, environmental and linguistic characteristics of Wales. Examples are to be drawn from Wales at Key Stage 1 and at Key Stage 2 two of the three studies of places should be within Wales.

Design and technology

This is a newly conceptualized subject which combines designing and making skills with knowledge and understanding of materials, mechanisms, uses and products. There are three attainment targets: 'designing', 'making' and 'knowledge and understanding'.

At Key Stage 1 pupils should work on practical tasks to develop skills at designing and making simple products. They should investigate, make, disassemble and evaluate products and work with a wide range of materials. They should begin to develop a sense of a design process in which ideas are initiated, developed, applied and the results evaluated. They should be taught about simple mechanisms, structures, products and applications, quality and health and safety, and the vocabulary to talk and think about them.

At Key Stage 2 pupils' opportunities should be extended and they should be taught further designing skills and making skills. For instance, their design should be more thorough and focused and their making skills should be more precise and controlled in the use and finishing of materials. Evaluations should be more refined. Pupils' knowledge and understanding should be extended too in respect of mechanisms, structures, products and applications, quality and health and safety, and the vocabulary to describe and evaluate design processes and products.

For assessment purposes, there are level descriptions describing characteristic pupil attainments for each of the three attainment targets in design and technology.

Information technology (IT)

Given its importance in modern life, this curriculum area is newly specified as a free-standing subject in the revised National Curriculum. There is a single attainment target in the programme of study: 'information technology'.

At Key Stage 1 pupils should be given opportunities 'to use a variety of IT equipment and software including microcomputers and various kinds of software'. At the simplest levels, pupils should be taught to communicate and handle information using IT and ways of controlling and modelling using IT. For instance, they might consider the function of everyday devices such as a toaster or electric model.

At Key Stage 2 the application of IT should begin to spread across different subjects and understanding and confidence in use of IT should be developed. Ways of communicating and handling information should become more sophisticated and IT equipment should be used to monitor events as well as for control and modelling. Control equipment should begin to be used for experimentation, prediction and testing.

For assessment purposes, there are level descriptions describing characteristic pupil attainments for the information technology attainment target.

Art

Art is a subject which has often been used in the primary curriculum in the context of topic work. For example, to express or represent understanding in the humanities. However, the National Curriculum has asserted its place as a subject of study, as well as of expression. In particular, the highlighting of 'visual literacy' through the 'visual elements' is important. In the National Curriculum, art is taken to embrace art, craft and design. There are two attainment targets within the programme of study for art: 'investigating and making', and 'knowledge and understanding'.

At Key Stage 1 pupils should experiences different approaches to art, craft and design and develop visual perception through expression of feelings, recording of artefacts and design. They should experiment with techniques. They should begin to develop an understanding of visual literacy in relation to pattern and texture, colour, images using line and tone and the use of shape, form and space. They should be introduced to the work of artists, craft workers and designers to 'develop their appreciation of the richness of our diverse cultural heritage'.

At Key Stage 2 children's work should be extended. They should have more opportunities to work in different media and with different approaches to art, developing their visual perception and practical skills though expressive experiences, observational recording and the collection of visual evidence. Experimentation with different techniques and media should develop pupils' understanding of visual elements, such as line, tone, colour, shape, to make images and artefacts for different purposes. In studying the work of artists, children should identify how visual elements are used for particular purposes and they should begin to respond to, and evaluate, art.

For assessment purposes, there are end of Key Stage descriptions describing characteristic pupil attainments which pupils should have reached in respect of each art attainment target.

In Wales, pupils are to be given opportunities to develop and apply their knowledge and understanding of the cultural, economic, environmental and linguistic characteristics of Wales. Art is structured by three attainment targets: understanding, making and investigating and there is reference to the work of Welsh artists.

Music

Music is a subject which has always been important in primary schools, contributing to communal activities in class and school performances. The National Curriculum emphasizes musical experience and draws attention to 'musical elements' of pitch, duration, dynamics, tempo, timbre, texture and structure.

There are two attainment targets within the programme of study for music: 'performing and composing' and 'listening and appraising'.

At Key Stage 1 children should be taught to sing songs, play simple musical pieces, rehearse and share in music-making, improvise, explore and create simple musical structures and communicate their ideas to others. They should learn to listen to different kinds of simple music and to develop understanding of it, and to respond and evaluate their own, and others', music.

At Key Stage 2 children's musical learning should develop further producing more understanding and control of the musical elements. For instance, they should develop more diction in their singing, sing with others in two parts, improvise, use patterns and structures of sounds to achieve effects and record their compositions using notation where appropriate. They should develop their listening, appreciation and criteria for responding to and appraising music, so that they can express ideas and use musical knowledge to support their arguments.

For assessment purposes, there are end of Key Stage descriptions describing characteristic pupil attainments which pupils should have reached in respect of each music attainment target.

In Wales pupils are to be given opportunities to develop and apply their knowledge and understanding of the cultural, economic, environmental and linguistic characteristics of Wales. Music is structured by three attainment targets: performing, composing and appraising and there is reference to the work of Welsh music and traditions.

Physical education (PE)

Physical education is important for children's physical development and, because of the activity, is often very popular with many children. The National Curriculum requires the promotion of physical activity and healthy lifestyles, positive attitudes and safe practices in PE. There is one attainment target within the programme of study for physical education: 'physical education'.

At Key Stage 1 there are three areas of activity to be taught. Games involves simple competitive games both as individuals and as small groups, ways of sending, receiving and travelling with a ball and developing movement in games through running, chasing, etc. Gymnastic activities are different ways of travelling on hands and feet, such as rolling, jumping, balancing, etc. Dance involves control, co-ordination, balance, poise and elevation and the performance of simple dances, including some traditional ones. Moods and feelings should be explored through dance using different rhythms and speeds, shapes, directions and levels.

At Key Stage 2 there are six areas of activity to be taught. Games skills are to be developed so that small-scale competitive team games are played, including those involving attack and defence in invasion. Gymnastics is to be developed and refined to extend sequences of movement on both floor and apparatus. Dance is also to be extended in terms of composition and control, experience of dance forms and the expression of feelings, moods and ideas. Athletic activities regarding techniques in running, throwing and jumping are to be developed, and measurement and comparison of own performances is to be made. Outdoor and adventurous activities, such as orienteering and others with a physical challenge, are to be performed in safe locations. Finally, confidence at swimming by a variety of means is to be developed, including the capability to swim unaided for at least 25 metres and the principles of water safety.

For assessment purposes, there is an end of Key Stage description describing characteristic pupil attainments which pupils should have reached in respect of the physical education attainment target.

References

Alexander, R., Rose, J. and Woodhead, C. (1992) *Curriculum Organisation and Classroom Practice in Primary Schools: A Discussion Paper.* London: DES.

Audit Commission (1991) *Management within the Primary School.* London: HMSO.

Ball, S. J. (1990) *Politics and Policy Making in Education.* London: Routledge.

Barrett, G. (1986) *Starting School, An Evaluation of the Experience.* London: AMMA.

Bennett, N. (1987) 'The search for the effective primary school teacher', in Delamont, S. (ed.) *The Primary School Teacher.* London: Falmer.

Bennett, N. (1994) *Class Size in Primary Schools.* London: Joint Class Size Steering Group.

Bennett, N. and Dunne, E. (1992) *Managing Classroom Groups.* London: Cassell.

Bennett, N. and Kell, J. (1989) *A Good Start? Four Year Olds in Infant Schools.* Oxford: Blackwell.

Bernstein, B. (1975) *Class, Codes and Control, Volume 3: Towards a Theory of Educational Transmission.* London: Routledge and Kegan Paul.

Blenkin, G. V. and Kelly, A. V. (eds) (1993) *The Primary Curriculum in Action.* London: Harper and Row.

Blyth, A. (1984) *Development, Experience and Curriculum in Primary Education.* London: Croom Helm.

Board of Education (1931) *Report of the Consultative Committee on the Primary School*, (The Hadow Report). London: HMSO.

Bruner, J. S. (1990) *Acts of Meaning.* London: Harvard University Press.

Bullock Report (1975) *A Language for Life.* London: HMSO.

Caldwell, B. and Spinks, J. (1988) *The Self-Managing School*. London: Falmer.

Campbell, R. J. and Neill, S. R. St. J. (1994) *Primary Teachers at Work*. London: Routledge.

Central Advisory Council for Education (1967) *Children and their Primary Schools* (The Plowden Report). London: CACE.

Clegg, D. and Billington, S. (1994), *The Effective Primary Classroom*. London: David Fulton.

Cockcroft Report (1982) *Mathematics Counts*. London: HMSO.

Cortazzi, M. (1990) *Primary Teaching: How it Is*. London: David Fulton.

Council of Europe (1985) *Teaching and Learning about Human Rights in Primary Schools*. (Recommendation no. R(85)7 of the Committee of Ministers; Council of Europe, Strasbourg).

David, T. (1993) *Primary Teachers, Parents and Governors*. Stoke-on-Trent: Trentham.

Davies, B. (1982) *Life in the Classroom and Playground*. London: Routledge.

Delamont, S. (ed.) (1987) *The Primary School Teacher*. London: Falmer.

Department for Education (1994) *Our Children's Education: The Updated Parent's Charter*. London: Department for Education.

Department for Education (1994) *School Governors: A Guide to the Law*. London: Department for Education.

Department of Education and Science, (1989) *National Curriculum: From Policy to Practice*. London: Department of Education and Science.

Drummond, M. J. (1993) *Assessing Children's Learning*. London: David Fulton.

Early Years Curricular Group (1989) *Early Childhood Education*. Stoke-on-Trent: Trentham.

Edwards, V. and Redfern, A. (1988) *At Home in School: Parent Participation in Primary Education*. London: Routledge.

Elton Report (1989) *Discipline in Schools*. London: HMSO.

Emerson, C. and Goddard, I. (1989) *All About the National Curriculum*. London: Heinemann.

Fullan, M. and Hargreaves, A. (1992) *What's Worth Fighting for in Your School? Working Together for Improvement.* Milton Keynes: Open University Press.

Goodnow, J. and Burns, A, (1985) *Home and School, A Child's Eye View*. London: Allen and Unwin.

Hannon, P. (1995) *Literacy, Home and School: Research and Practice in Teaching Literacy with Parents*. London: Falmer.

Hargreaves, D. and Hopkins, D. (1991) *The Empowered School*. London: Cassell.

Her Majesty's Chief Inspector of Schools (1995) *Standards and Quality in Education in 1993/4, The Report of HMCI*. London: OFSTED.

Her Majesty's Inspectors (1985) *The Curriculum from 5–16*. London: HMI.

Her Majesty's Inspectors (1987) *Primary Schools: Some Aspects of Good Practice*. London: HMSO.

Holt, J. (1965) *How Children Fail*. Harmondsworth: Penguin.

Holt, J. (1967) *How Children Learn*. Harmondsworth: Penguin.

House of Commons Select Committee on Education (1986) *Achievement in Primary Schools*. London: HMSO.

House of Commons Select Committee on Education (1994) *The Disparity in Funding between Primary and Secondary Schools*. London: HMSO.

Hughes, M., Wikeley, F. and Nash, T. *Parents and their Children's Schools*. Oxford: Blackwell.

Incomes Data Services (1992) *Hours and Holidays 1992*, Study 517. London: IDS.

Jackson, B. (1979) *Starting School*. London: Croom Helm.

Meyer, J. W., Kamens, D. H. and Benavot, A. (1992) *School Knowledge for the Masses*. London: Falmer.

McNamara, D. (1994) *Classroom Pedagogy and Primary Practice*. London: Routledge.

Mortimore, P., Sammons, P., Stoll, L., Lewis, D. and Ecob, R. (1988) *School Matters*. Wells: Open Books.

Mortimore, P. and Mortimore, J. (1991) *The Primary Head: Roles, Responsibilities and Reflections*. London: Chapman.

Munn, P. (ed.) (1993) *Parents and Schools: Customers, Managers or Partners?* London: Routledge.

National Oracy Project (1990) *Teaching, Talking and Learning at Key Stage One.* York: NCC.

Nias, J. (1989) *Primary Teachers Talking.* London: Routledge.

Nias, J., Southworth, G. and Yeomans, R. (1989) *Staff Relationships in the Primary School.* London: Cassell.

OFSTED (1995) *Handbook: Guidance in the Inspection of Nursery and Primary Schools.* HMSO London: OFSTED.

OFSTED (1994) *Improving Schools.* London: HMSO.

Osborn, M, (1996) 'Changes in teachers' professional perspectives at Key Stage 1', in Croll, P. (ed.) *Teachers, Pupils and Classrooms in Primary Education.* London: Cassell.

Paley, V. G. (1981) *Wally's Stories.* London: Harvard University Press.

Paley, V. G. (1990) *The Boy Who Would be a Helicopter.* London: Harvard University Press .

Patten, J. (1994) Secretary of State's comments at a press conference launch of new DfE circulars on league tables of school performance.

Pollard, A. (1985) *The Social World of the Primary School.* London: Cassell.

Pollard, A. (ed.) (1994) *Look Before You Leap? Research Evidence on the Impact of the National Curriculum at Key Stage Two.* London: Tufnell Press.

Pollard, A. with Filer, A. (1995) *The Social World of Children's Learning.* London: Cassell.

Pollard, A. and Filer, A. (1996) *The Social World of Pupil Careers.* London: Cassell.

Pollard, A. and Tann, S. (1993) *Reflective Teaching in the Primary School.* London: Cassell (second edition).

Pollard, A., Broadfoot, P., Croll, P., Osborn, M. and Abbott, D. (1994) *Changing English Primary Schools? The Impact of the Education Reform Act at Key Stage One.* London: Cassell.

Pountney, G. (1993) *Primary School Management.* London: Cassell.

Pring, R. (1995) *The New Curriculum.* London: Cassell (second edition).

Rowland, S. (1987) 'Child in Control: Towards an Interpretive Model of Teaching and Learning', in A. Pollard (ed.) *Children and Their Primary Schools*. London: Falmer Press.

Sallis, J. (1994) *Heads and Governors: Building the Partnership*. London: Routledge.

Shephard, G. (1994) Secretary of State's speech to NUT Conference, Easter.

Slukin, A. (1981) *Growing Up in the Playground*. London: Croom Helm.

Taylor, T. (1977) *A New Partnership for Our Schools* (The Taylor Report), London: HMSO.

Tizard, B. and Hughes, M. (1984) *Young Children Learning*. London: Fontana.

Warnock Report (1978) *Special Education: Forward Trends*. London: HMSO.

Wood, D. (1988) *How Children Think and Learn*. Oxford: Blackwell.

Woods, P. (1995) *Creative Teachers in Primary Schools*. Milton Keynes: Open University Press.

Wragg, E. C. and Partington, J. A. (1995) *The School Governors' Handbook*. London: Routledge.

Index